SOCIETY AND RELIGION DURING THE AGE OF INDUSTRIALIZATION:

CHRISTIANITY IN VICTORIAN ENGLAND

Lee E. Grugel

Moorhead State University

illustrated by Paul Duginski

University Press of America™

Library of Congress Catalog Card Number: 78-65844

For

Annie and Chris

Preface

Professor Owen Chadwick begins his superb two-volumed study, The Victorian Church (1966-1970), with an unusually plain statement. "Victorian England was religious". How true that statement is and yet the words beg for the careful elaboration which Chadwick, and many other scholars in recent years, have attempted to provide. Despite the interest in Victorian history generally and religion especially, many questions remain topics for continuing research and discussion. And as is often the case, the specialist and advanced student have been far better served than beginning scholars and the general reader to whom this book is principally addressed.

Victorian England. The term conjures up images of pious family gatherings, stern moral codes, serene country settings, ornate and heavy decoration, middle class ideas, power, empire, hypocrisy and so forth. During the middle and later years of the nineteenth century when Victoria occupied the throne, England* witnessed the creation of the modern industrial city. This was the age of the mature industrial revolution with its many consequences rippling through the British Isles and beyond through Europe and America to the rest of the world. From teeming London through the not so sleepy Cotswold villages to the hammering mill towns of the Midlands and industrial North, England was caught up in a process of unparalleled economic and social change. A more democratic political process evolved, vast wealth was created along with the blight and filth of slums; even the first halting steps were made towards erecting the institutions of the welfare society. It was a time of very rapid social transformation and, quite naturally, an age of self-judgement and criticism.

These were also years of very fundamental moral and spiritual crises for both individuals and groups. The physical and social adjustments required by industry were great indeed as old rural habits were forced to give way to urban behavior patterns. No less difficult was the religious adjustment because Englishmen of all ranks had, by the beginning of Victoria's reign, come to take their Christianity very seriously. New and troubling questions

---

*Although the term "Britain" which includes Scotland and Wales, will be used in this book, the focus will be mainly upon English affairs.

about the truth of Christian beliefs were raised by leading Victorian thinkers while, at the same time, the churches were forced to deal with new social situations.

These issues were vitally important and were not the concern only of the small percentage of Victorians who had a formal theological education. The Victorians were a highly literate people and quite ordinary folk took an active interest in religious concerns. They expressed their minds about moral issues, worried about their churches and, most importantly, about the ultimate destiny of human beings. The Christian churches in Europe had been presented with serious problems before--in the Reformation, the Scientific Revolution of the seventeenth century and the Enlightenment. The issues faced by Victorian Christians were no less formidable.

Scholars from many disciplines have re-examined Victorian history, partly due to their awareness that older conclusions needed revision and also, one suspicions, out of the belief that the problems which first were confronted by the Victorians are yet with us. Although the Victorians certainly had their faults, they approached life with the serious care and intelligence which commands admiration.

It is my hope that this book will serve as an introduction to an important and fascinating area of historical study. Even a small volume such as this one could not have been written without the assistance and encouragement of many people. Moorhead State University granted a much appreciated sabbatical leave and Manchester College, Oxford, provided a very appropriate setting in which to work. Martin Marty, Professor of Modern Church History, University of Chicago, who kindly read and critiqued the manuscript, generated my interest in Victorian Christianity. Ms. Marilyn Jenson and Ms. Connie Harper both provided highly competent secretarial support. The illustrations were done especially for this book by Mr. Paul Duginski. Lastly and most specially, Fran Grugel receives my thanks for her questions and many editorial suggestions. Errors of fact or judgement are, of course, my sole responsibility.

L.G.

Contents

CHAPTER I. VICTORIAN ENGLAND: WORKSHOP OF THE WORLD

The Age of Revolutions

"Revolutionary" is a term which has become all too readily applied to things or events which appear to be in any way out of the ordinary. Nevertheless it is with good reason that the last several decades of the eighteenth century have been called revolutionary. During those years rapid and drastic changes took place, affecting nearly everyone who lived in Western Europe and North America. Among historians it is commonly accepted that three major revolutions occurred.

Beginning in 1775, the American colonies, with timely help from France, conducted a successful war of national liberation against England. A new national government was soon established and a written constitution, incorporating most of the more advanced political ideas of the time, was ratified. Although historians will continue to argue about the precise nature of those events and the motivations of the men who carried them out, there is no question that the Americans had begun a daring and even noble experiment in self-government.

If historians are somewhat reluctant to characterize the American experience as revolutionary, they do not hesitate for a moment to so label the events which took place in France beginning in 1789. Not only were the political institutions of the old regime demolished but the entire structure of society was also radically altered. The representatives of the French people met in the Estates General in May to deal mainly with the immediate financial crisis facing the government.[1] Pent up social grievances and new political ideas prepared the way for high political drama. Before the summer of 1789 was over the delegates had formed a "National Assembly" and had abolished hereditary privileges of the aristocrats. Acting in the name of all Frenchmen, the Assembly took steps to limit the absolute power of the king and, most dramatically, proclaimed to the world a belief in human equality by the Declaration of the Rights of Man and of the Citizen. It is surely one of the great tragedies of history that

---

[1] This assembly composed of representatives of the French clergy, nobility and Third Estate (everyone not included in the other two categories) had not met since 1614.

1

these stirring actions in the cause of freedom became, in the space of a few years, associated with the terror of the guillotine and later were followed by the dictatorship of Napoleon. But the French Revolution, even more so than the American, stimulated a desire for democratic institutions, social equality and national independence: goals to which people the world over have aspired ever since.

England did not experience such political upheavals. (A good many people, like Edmund Burke in his <u>Reflections on the French Revolution</u> of 1790, were worried that a revolution might happen in England.) However an even more fundamental revolutionary experience was in progress. Political and social goals do motivate behavior but human beings have a more fundamental range of needs: food, clothing, adequate shelter, etc. To such basic necessities the Industrial Revolution addressed itself.

The Industrial Revolution was a complex series of related economic and social developments but it can be simply defined as those rapid changes which occurred in the methods for producing the things which people both needed and wanted. It is impossible, of course, to assign dates to the Industrial Revolution with the precision of the political revolutions of the time. Since ancient times, with the aid only of their muscles, animals and a few simple tools, people had converted natural resources to their use. The level of productivity had always been low. Only a small percentage of people in any area--the political, social and educated elite--could live in any degree of comfort. In all preindustrial societies the vast majority of people, then as now, had sufficient diets and inadequate shelter. Birth rates were high but few lived to adulthood. During the Industrial Revolution new machines were invented and small groups of craftsmen were replaced by complex associations of owners, workers and distributors. In short, human beings were placed into a new relationship with nature and with each other. The Industrial Revolution opened up possibilities for a better life that could not be offered by even the most visionary of political revolutionaries.

The Industrial Revolution in England

Why was England the first nation to experience industrialization? Economists list land, labor and capital or tools as the necessary factors of production. Subtract any one and production ceases altogether. Sometimes a fourth factor, entrepreneurship--the act of bringing the other three factors together in the right combination--is also included. In each of these categories, eighteenth century England had distinct advantages over other countries; in a word, England was "ripe" for rapid economic growth.

Labor and land are two very related factors. At the time of the first national census of 1801 the population of England and Wales stood at approximately nine million. A century earlier, it was probably less than six million. During the eighteenth century population had begun to increase because of a small but important decline in the death rate among infants. It does not appear that there were improvements in medical care or sanitation which allowed more children to survive. It is certain, however, that land was being more efficiently utilized thus increasing available food supplies. Although really dramatic improvements in agriculture would not come until well into the nineteenth century, English landowners had been working with new crops, improving their livestock by experimental breeding and enclosing or fencing tracts of land which also led to greater efficiency. By increasing the food supply, one of the natural checks on population growth--inadequate diet--was reduced with the important result that population increased at a significant rate.

The fact of a larger population had several effects on the English economy. First there was a greater demand for products which led some producers, although the old craft guilds resisted, to search for the means to increase production and, of course, their profits as well. Additionally, because the population could not all be employed in agriculture, the cost of labor was kept low as more people competed for available work. Nevertheless, an abundant supply of workers and the demand for goods were not sufficient conditions for an industrial revolution. Even if one recognizes the considerable quantities of natural resources-- wool, iron and coal--located in such a small country, at least two other conditions were needed to be present before industrial- ization could commence.

First, capital or money was necessary to bring workers, materials and machines together. Landowners, commercial men, bankers and even tradesmen had accumulated money from a variety of sources during the eighteenth century. Capital was generated by agriculture, foreign and colonial trade, domestic industries such as brewing and pottery, and from tolls collected on roads and canals. This money was often poured into elegantly furnished country homes. But many Englishmen, particularly those heirs of the Puritans, looked at wealth not merely as a means of grati- fying their wants but as a gift from God to be used wisely and

profitably.[2] Saving and investment were natural economic consequences. Without such funds to be ventured in new enterprises,
very limited growth could have taken place.

Secondly, the Industrial Revolution is invariably associated
with the manufacture of cotton cloth, a product which rapidly
replaced wool as the major textile commodity. The flying shuttle
had been invented by John Kay (1704-1764) earlier in the eighteenth
century; spinning machines developed by Richard Arkwright (1732-
1792), Samuel Crompton (1753-1827) and James Hargreaves (d. 1778)
were all being used during the 1780s. In 1784, Edmund Cartwright
(1743-1823) patented a loom which could be driven by water power
and, soon after this breakthrough, James Watt (1736-1819) made
improvements on the steam engine rendering it capable of driving
other machinery. Watt's business partner, Matthew Boulton (1728-
1809) described the demand for power sources. In 1781 he wrote,
"The people in London, Manchester and Birmingham are steam mill
mad." These developments, combined with the increased cotton
production in the American South, created a boom in the textile
industry. In turn, other new and important industries such as
mining, the metal trades and transportation were stimulated. In
the Midlands and the North of England especially, factories grew
and towns which had been rural villages since medieval times
became congested urban centers.

It is possible, of course, to overdramatize such events.
Rural England still existed and does exist even today. Old manu-
facturing techniques continued to be employed for many years and
most early factories were small by modern standards. But for
millions of English, Scots and Welsh people the Industrial Revolution constituted unprecedented social change. The structure
of society, British political and cultural institutions--espe-
cially the churches--would all be greatly affected by the new
economic conditions.

The Social Consequences of Industrialization

The people whose lives, at least initially, were only mod-
erately affected by economic change were those at the very top of

---

[2]So much has been written about the relationship between
capitalism and the Protestant Ethic that nothing need be added
here. One of the most important works is R.H. Tawney, Religion
and the Rise of Capitalism (1926).

society, the gentlemen and large landowners. New opportunities were opened for investment and there were many new mouths to be fed with the produce from their estates. These landowners still controlled the political system and they secured a substantial measure of economic security for themselves in 1815 when Parliament passed a series of acts known as the Corn Laws, tariffs which kept the price of grain from falling below a certain level thus protecting the fortunes of gentlemen and farmers. Although they derived benefits from industrialization, the landowners often deplored the new and ugly factory towns and denounced the liberal ideas undergirding capitalism. They even worried about the disappearance of the rural landscape. It would not be until near the end of the nineteenth century, however, that large landholders would see their fortunes and social prestige seriously eroded by the Industrial Revolution.

From the time of the Middle Ages there had been a middle class in England consisting of shopkeepers, craftsmen, scholars and commercial people. Whenever possible they sought to acquire real estate and to emulate the ways of gentlemen. During the Industrial Revolution members of the middle class provided investment capital, inventions and entrepreneurial skills. A few made considerable fortunes but it is incorrect to think of these early manufacturers as captains of industry, living in luxury like the great industrial magnates of later years. The threat of failure was always near. The owner often worked beside his employee in the early factories, and many factory operators treated their "hands" with respect, especially in the more skilled occupations. However, in the larger more impersonal operations, the Lancashire textile mills or Northumberland coal fields for example, workers might be driven to the limits of physical endurance. Humanitarian considerations were eclipsed by economic necessity as entrepreneurs became increasingly committed to the concepts of free competition and unrestricted trade which had been formulated by economists such as Adam Smith in his treatise, The Wealth of Nations (1776). This middle class did accumulate wealth but they continued to lack one important possession, however, the political power to accompany and to protect their advanced economic status.

It is to that new class created by the Industrial Revolution, the urbanized factory workers, that many historians have given their attention. Men and their families flocked from the countryside, lured by the promises of higher wages, to the new and dismal slums of factory cities like Manchester, Leeds and Birmingham. Their lives were often wretched beyond belief.

Long hours, pitifully low wages, hazardous working conditions and the threat of unemployment were all to be part of their new life. Death rates in the factory towns, as well as birth rates, remained at high levels through much of the nineteenth century.

Because of low wages it was often necessary for every member of the laboring family to seek employment. The most deplorable feature of early industrialization was the exploitation of women and children in textile mills and coal mines. Reporting to a Parliamentary Commission on Children's Employment in 1842, Sarah Gooder, aged eight years, spoke of her work as a trapper (a person who opened doors in the shafts to allow coal cars to pass) in the mines.

> I'm a trapper in the Gauber Pit. I have to trap without a light, and I'm scared. I go at four and sometimes halfpast, I never go to sleep. Sometimes I sing when I've light, but not in the dark; I dare not sing then. I don't like being in the pit. I am very sleepy when I go sometimes in the morning.

Although wages were low and working conditions very bad, the most difficult adjustment for people to make was to the nature of factory routine and discipline. Work was strictly regulated by the clock or factory whistle. Although labor in rural England was by no means easy or pleasant, the pace had always been leisurely. Even more importantly there was even less security now than before against hard times because the traditional system of welfare virtually collapsed under the pressures of population growth.

Since 1600, Poor Laws had required property owners in each parish (the smallest unit of government) to tax themselves to provide for those who were unable to work either because of some personal handicap or because of general unemployment. The poor were either given small sums of money or provided with a job. No such social security, minimal though it had been, was afforded the worker in early industrial England. Private charities were few and could not deal with the needs of a greatly enlarged population. Furthermore, it was a common belief among the members of the middle classes that wages could never rise above the level of subsistence; the working class man, woman or child was considered to be bound by an "iron law" of low wages.

During prosperous times the factory laborer might receive a living wage. However when the great war with Napoleonic France

6

ended in 1815, demand slackened and factories were forced to reduce production. In many cases business operations failed; unemployment reached peak levels. The government meanwhile seemed utterly hostile to demands to alleviate the terrible situation. When workingmen gathered at St. Peter's Fields in Manchester in 1819 to listen to a radical political speech by Henry Hunt, violence erupted. Eleven people were killed and hundreds wounded as the local militia attempted to disburse the crowd. Finding himself in a desperate situation, the barely literate workingman sometimes took drastic action. One group, the Luddites, resorted to wrecking the machines themselves to prevent the loss of their jobs. However the more sophisticated spokesmen of the working classes had concluded, like the middle class, that political power was the best solution to their difficulty.

Political Consequences of Industrialization

Population growth and an altered distribution of wealth was to have a significant impact on British political activity throughout the nineteenth century. Since the middle ages, the structure of government had been slowly evolving with dramatic changes taking place periodically as, for example, during the Civil War and revolutions of the seventeenth century. Although there was no written constitution, important political documents, beginning with Magna Carta of 1215, served to define the nature of government. By the early nineteenth century the supremacy of Parliament had become clearly established. The monarch had not yet been reduced to figurehead status, but real authority lay with the Prime Minister and the members of his cabinet. In turn their power rested on maintaining support for their policies by a majority of members in the House of Commons. Before any bill could become law it had to be passed by both the House of Commons and the House of Lords.[3] Because the House of Commons had come to control finances and appropriations it was by far the most important component of the system.

---

[3] In 1830 there were 658 members of the House of Commons. 100 sat for Ireland, 45 for Scotland, and the remainder represented constituencies in England and Wales. The Lords included Peers of the Realm (nobility) and Anglican bishops. The number varied but approximately 360 votes were cast in the Lords on the Reform Bill of 1832.

Two political parties existed, the Whigs and the Tories, along with a sprinkling of those who called themselves Radicals. Unlike modern British parties, these groups were not tied to any clearly defined ideology and they lacked discipline. The Tories generally represented the conservative elements, especially the small rural landholders, while the Whigs tended to represent commercial interests.

In terms of real power, the landed classes and old established families could still call the political tunes in 1830. Nevertheless, population changes coupled with economic crises and with the increasingly widespread notion that governments should be more broadly representative resulted in demands to reform the House of Commons. The Tory party, led by the hero of Waterloo, the Duke of Wellington (1769-1852), was in power and they had carried out several major reforms in the late 1820s such as the Repeal of the Test and Corporation Acts and Catholic Emancipation (See below, Chapter 2). But the Tories balked at changing the method of representation.

Middle class reformers based their demands for change on the idea that government--indeed any institution or law--should serve the greatest good of the greatest number of people. Known as the Utilitarian Principle, this concept had been framed initially by the eccentric but brilliant Jeremy Bentham (1748-1831) in his Principles of Morals and Legislation (1789). Common sense also dictated that the manner of election and mode of representation were drastically out of step with current reality. No change had taken place for centuries. There had been earlier attempts to achieve parliamentary reform but these had always been squashed because of the fear that even minor changes could signal the beginning of revolution.

By 1832 the immediate threat of violent social disruption had been reduced. The Whigs had been able to gain a majority in the House of Commons in 1830. After two years of vigorous activity in both Parliament and the nation as a whole (there were a few cases of threats and violence, especially when the Lords refused to pass the bill) the Great Reform Bill became law. It was one of the most important documents in British constitutional development. This Reform Bill was in no way a radical measure. In the House of Commons, seats were taken away from boroughs (towns which sent members to Parliament) which had lost population and given to those areas where population had increased. Secondly, the qualifications for voting were made uniform throughout Britain.

The right to vote was based on the amount of land held or assessed tax value of property. Although the bill can not be said to have been democratic--still only 600,000 or about one person in twenty-one could vote--it did set a precedent for further changes.

The Reform Bill satisfied the middle classes because their interests could now be adequately represented. A few workingmen, if they had sufficient income, could also vote but the vast majority of laborers remained disenfranchised. The effectiveness of this bill was soon to be tested by renewed economic crisis. Would the government, now that it was more widely representative, be more responsive to the needs of the majority of the people?

This bill was not the only major piece of legislation to be achieved by the middle classes during the 1830s and 1840s. The Poor Law was amended in 1834 in such a way as to make the recipients of welfare feel great social disapproval. Impoverished families were packed off to workhouses in which the living conditions were often very degrading. Although this new Poor Law was a harsh measure it did conform both to the Utilitarian test of a good law and to the prevailing notion that individual laziness, rather than social conditions, was the cause of poverty.

In opposition to agricultural interests the Corn Laws were repealed in 1846. By this action, Parliament demonstrated the new political power of the middle classes. Of less satisfaction to industrialists were the Factory Acts passed to control the hours of labor, especially for women and children. Because these laws provided for government inspection of factories, they were disliked by the owners who defended their unrestricted business freedom. Without question the 1830s and 1840s were extremely significant decades in British political development, but legislative activity alone did little to relieve those suffering under the burdens of early industrialization.

For the laboring classes, the late 1830s and the 1840s was a time of severe economic hardship. Unemployment was often at high levels and, although strikes were legalized, they seldom were successful in raising wages or bettering working conditions. Frustration and class antagonism increased among factory workers because the House of Commons responded no more readily to their plight than it had done before the Reform Act of 1832. What was most lacking was the social and economic security which, as many workers had come to believe, true democracy would guarantee.

Building on the political traditions begun in the last century by radicals like Tom Paine (1737-1809), working class spokesmen, with the aid of a few middle class radicals, attempted to bring a further measure of reform to the House of Commons. In 1838 a great petition or Charter was drawn up demanding universal manhood suffrage, annual elections, the absolute equalization of electoral districts and other features to make the House of Commons a representative institution. The Charter obtained millions of signatures and was presented to Parliament three times--in 1839, 1842, and 1848. It had no chance of being accepted because it was too democratic, too far ahead of its time. The House of Commons rejected it by large majorities on each occasion. Although a few Chartist leaders advocated violent retaliation, their campaigns and protests were usually peaceful. The immediate goal of the Chartists seemed to be political representation, but the working classes were actually searching for a means to achieve economic security.

An alternative course was to ignore political action altogether. The Owenites, or Socialists as they were commonly called, believed that no amount of political tinkering could create a just society. In his younger years, Robert Owen (1771-1858) had been a successful textile manufacturer. He had also come to hold the opinion that a person's character was formed by his environment, a conviction which led Owen to reject the ethics of individualism and competition. What he and his disciples attempted to bring about was a fundamental reformation of society. In their "new moral world," competitive values would be replaced by cooperative behavior.

Owen's message had a powerful appeal but very little in the way of practical results was accomplished. Several cooperative communities were founded but all failed within a few years. Nevertheless the Owenites had diagnosed fundamental weaknesses of early capitalism. Competition did often lead to social chaos and the fact that one person worked only on another's material did result in dehumanization. By the end of the 1840s, however, both Chartism and Owenism had lost much of their earlier popularity.

Developments During the Later Nineteenth Century

Something of an economic miracle took place in Britain around the middle of the nineteenth century. By this time, Britain really had become the workshop of the world. The nation's technological and industrial supremacy was symbolized in the Great

10

Exhibition held in a gigantic hall of glass, the Crystal Palace, in 1851. On display were items from around the world but the exhibits which attracted most comment were the products of British technology.

The coming of the railways in the 1840s stimulated the economy and reduced unemployment. Thousands were employed in construction and products could now be marketed more cheaply because transportation costs were reduced. Between 1850 and the middle of the 1870s, the British economy flourished and all classes benefitted. Pockets of extreme poverty remained but the worst of the industrial abuses had been eliminated. Higher wage levels led to higher standards of living. The edge of political protest was blunted not only by the strong economy but also by the widespread acceptance of middle class ideas of individualism and self-help among the skilled laborers.

These economic gains were also followed by political progress for the workingmen. In 1867, the Second Reform Bill passed the House of Commons. It doubled the size of the voting public and included almost all urban workingmen. During these years the number of hours in the working week declined, public transportation became available to the masses of people and education was improved. On the surface, times could not have been better. There were some sensitive observers, like Matthew Arnold (1822-1888), who proclaimed the lack of a true culture in the new industrial society. The most popular writer of the age was Charles Dickens whose novels portrayed, often in comic relief, every flaw to be found in the middle class character. Nevertheless the British people had become accustomed to the industrial way of life.

These prosperous years were not to last. Never again would England experience the severe economic maladjustment of the early industrial period but bad harvests in the 1870s and increasing foreign competition from Germany and the United States did depress the economy. Economic historians have spoken of the "Great Depression", stretching over the last thirty years of the nineteenth century. Although both Europe and America were effected, it was not as catastrophic as the terrible depression which was yet to come in the 1930s.

In Britain, wages tended to stabilize, profits leveled off and sometimes declined and expressions of class antagonism were again heard in the land. A few British intellectuals became

11

attracted to the ideas of Karl Marx but the majority who became Socialists believed that wealth could be redistributed and collectivized by peaceful means. Workingmen increasingly felt that their interests were represented by neither major political party, Liberal or Conservative (heirs of the Whigs and Tories). The foundations of the modern Labour Party were laid during these years.

Events were also taking place beyond the shores of Britain which attracted much public attention. First, there was the eternal question of Ireland. Since 1800, Ireland had been governed directly by Parliament. Irish nationalist organizations, the existence of a solid block of Irish representatives in the House of Commons and the moral concerns felt by William Gladstone (1809-1898), three times Prime Minister and the leader of the Liberal Party, all combined to raise the issue of Irish independence in the mid-1880s. Because a large minority of the Liberal Party, fearing Catholic domination of the Protestant minority in a free Ireland, was hostile to Home Rule, the Liberal Party was seriously fractured.

But it was possible to look further than Ireland and to be greeted by far more gratifying sights for England was again enlarging her empire. Ever since the conclusion of the American War of Independence, there had been a rather negative view of colonial possessions. Although the vast nation of India, acquired in the eighteenth century, was retained, colonial ties were thought to be a hindrance rather than a help to trade. In the 1870s Britain began an imperial course once again. This time the focus was on the continent of Africa. The leading spokesman in Parliament for an imperial policy was Benjamin Disraeli (1804-1881), Conservative Party leader and Prime Minister (1874-1880). "Dizzy" believed that Britain had to act like a great nation to be a great nation. He meant that Britain, like France, Germany and Italy, had to increase her colonial possessions. As a result of such policies, the majority of African territory and sizeable sections of Asia were claimed by Europeans as colonies. The motives behind these policies have been variously described. Some historians have seen colonial action as yet another move in the old political struggle among European nations. The interpretations which have stood analysis best attribute imperialist activity to economic factors.

Faced with diminishing natural resources and markets, commercial men, with the help of the state, sought new sources of supply and new consumers. The most interesting economic interpretation later to be adopted by Lenin, was put forth in 1902 by the British economist, J.A. Hobson (1858-1940). In his book, Imperialism, he sought to show how large holders of capital funds invested in underdeveloped areas because they could get a much greater return on their investments. The government protected their money and the rest of the nation supported imperialism for a variety of humanitarian and even scientific motives.

Imperialism has been rightly judged as exploitative. It is, however, also true that many British men and women often sacrificed their lives in remote and primitive places not for profit but as doctors, teachers and missionaries. If the political and economic side of colonialism is condemnable, the accounts should partially be balanced by considering the more positive aspects of native contact with European peoples.

By the beginning of the twentieth century, adult Englishmen and women had come to live in a vastly new and changed world. Although prosperity had eventually come for most people it had not necessarily brought contentment. No one living in 1900 could see what terrible years were to come for Britain and the rest of Europe in the twentieth century. Yet in spite of a good deal of surface gaiety people were deeply troubled.

Members of the upper class could still amuse themselves with frivolous pastimes. They did, however, come to realize that the world over which they could easily rule was gone forever. Middle class youths, from the children of wealthy industrialists to the office clerks and secretaries, believed that their lives lacked significant challenge. In a sense they welcomed the news of increasing international tension. The nineteenth century had been an age of peace, perhaps a good short war would bring adventure. The working classes had generally gained a level of economic well-being and security which would have been the envy of their grandparents. But they were well aware that people who worked only with their hands in Britain were still not really recognized as full and worthy members of their society.

In spite of the changes and nagging problems, there was one living monument of stability, the Queen. In 1897, Victoria celebrated the sixtieth year of her reign and then she lived on for another four years. Few of her subjects could remember when she was not their queen. In a curious way the old woman did symbolize England and even, before her death, the age had adopted her name.

13

Queen Victoria

"The king is dead. Long live the Queen!" Early in the morning of 20 June 1837 Alexandrina Victoria, daughter of the late Duke of Kent, was awakened with the news that her uncle, King William IV, was dead. Victoria was barely eighteen years old. To her diary she confided,

> Since it has pleased Providence to place me in this station, I shall do my utmost to fulfill my duty towards my country; I am very young, and perhaps in many, though not in all things, inexperienced, but I am sure that very few have more real good will and more real desire to do what is fit and right than I have.

No better choice for the new monarch could have been made.

In 1837 many Englishmen had lost respect for the very idea of monarchy. It seemed to be an enormous expenditure for one thing and the ideas of republicanism had become widespread among many reformers. But more than this, the last three kings had heaped discredit upon the throne. George III (1760-1820) was a narrow-minded despot and had been insane during the last ten years of his reign. His son, George IV (1820-1830) was notorious for his behavior; he drank heavily, told dirty stories in public, lived openly with mistresses and shocked the country by asking Parliament to be divorced from Queen Caroline. No one mourned his death. William IV (1830-1837) was little different. Although he paid more attention to affairs of state, he did nothing to restore any respect for the Crown. By contrast to her predecessors, young Victoria seemed to embody all that was virtuous. Had she followed the ways of her uncles it is probable that England today would not have a royal family. What sort of person was this young woman and what powers did she exercise in the realm?

Victoria was born on 24 May 1819. Less than a year later her father, the Duke of Kent, died. Victoria led an isolated life in childhood and became very attached to her German governess, Baroness Lehzen. Her education was thorough and consisted of languages, history, sports, music, dancing and the forms of etiquette expected of a princess. Victoria was not gifted with superior intelligence nor was she especially pretty but she was high-spirited and determined to complete the tasks required of her. During the early months of her reign, Victoria demonstrated her belief that she had a significant public responsibility by trying to select her own ministers, action which a strictly constitutional monarch does not usually take.

PRINCESS VICTORIA

There is no doubt whatever about the most significant personal events in her long life. The first was her marriage to her handsome German cousin, Albert. After meeting him on several occasions, Victoria herself made the marriage proposal because "he would never have presumed to take such a liberty" with the Queen of England. They were married on 10 February 1840. Almost immediately a change of character took place in Victoria. She was deeply in love with Albert and she placed great reliance on the opinions of her husband. Although Albert was initially looked upon as a foreigner, his capacity for political and scientific matters soon earned him a high reputation among the English.

The Royal couple presented the first generations of Victorian people with the image of complete respectability. Albert was industrious and business-like; Victoria was the devoted wife and mother. Their union resulted in the birth of nine children; the first, Victoria, was born in November, 1840 and the last, Beatrice, in 1857. Although Victoria revealed a particular distaste for child-bearing, there is no doubt about her consuming affection for Prince Albert. For Victoria, the world was nearly idyllic, and then, after twenty-one years of a growing dependency on Albert, tragedy struck. In late November, 1861, Prince Albert began to exhibit symptoms of the dreaded typhoid; his strength failed rapidly and on 14 December 1861, he was dead.

Victoria was nearly insane with grief. For the next forty years of her life she was in mourning for her husband. Whenever possible she secluded herself from her ministers. Her eldest son, the future Edward VII, did little by his indelicate behavior to ease his mother's sorrow. Although the memory of Albert would recede somewhat with time, Queen Victoria would never again be a happy woman although her reign would be marked by so many national achievements.

Although Victoria seldom went out into the kingdom over which she ruled and she gave little evidence that she understood political matters, her opinions had to be taken into consideration by the ten Prime Ministers between 1840 and 1901. Some, like Melbourne and Disraeli she respected, perhaps even had affection for. Others especially Gladstone, she despised; the rest she tolerated. And Victoria did have an almost intuitive awareness of her people. For the poor she had pity. After seeing the industrial slums in 1852 she wrote these impressions:

It is like another world. In the midst of so much wealth, there seems to be nothing but ruin. As far as the eye can

reach, one sees nothing but chimneys, flaming furnaces,
many deserted but not pulled down, with wretched cottages
around them. . . Add to this a thick and black atmosphere. . .
and you have a faint impression of the life. . which a third
of a million of my poor subjects are forced to lead. It
makes me sad.

Victoria was conservative by nature, perhaps longing for the
past when Britain was a rural land. Yet her political sympathies
lay with the hard-working and prosperous middle classes. She
understood them. Lord Salisbury giving his eulogy to Victoria
following her death said,

I always thought that when I knew what the Queen thought
I knew pretty certainly what view her subjects would take
and especially the middle classes of her subjects. Such
was the extraordinary penetration of her mind.

Although Salisbury perhaps gave too much credit to the Queen's
perceptive abilities there is no doubt that she was a respected
figure among the people. On both the fiftieth and sixtieth anni-
versaries of her coronation great celebrations brought millions of
subjects from throughout the empire to pay homage to Victoria. By
the end of her reign in 1901, Victoria was more than just a woman
who happened to be Queen; she had become an institution.

* * * * *

The history of England in the Victorian age of industrialization has often been told from an economic and political perspective. A great many scholars have drawn attention to the Victorian
writers and artists for this age produced a galaxy of critical and
probing observers. Dickens is the foremost name but George Bernard
Shaw, Alfred Lord Tennyson, William Morris, George Eliot, John
Ruskin, Matthew Arnold and Mrs. Gaskell also tell us much of the
character of the Victorian years. This list could be almost indef-
initely extended.

It is also appropriate to examine the changing world of the
Victorians from the perspective of their religious institutions
and beliefs. No institution was more central to the lives of the
people and none was more altered by the consequences of the Industrial Revolution then the Victorian Churches. Christian beliefs
and customs were shaken by science, democracy and the new conclusions
of Victorian social thinkers. Periods of great change in Western

Civilization have always been accompanied by religious crises. The Victorian world was certainly no exception. As the churches sought to meet the demands of urban industrial society, they not only reflected the new age but also helped to create its most distinctive character.

In Ages Past

The astonishing characteristic of English religion when Victoria came to the throne was not that it was Christian but that so many forms of Christianity existed. Although they were overwhelmingly Portestant, English Christians had, in the three centuries since the Reformation, become divided over questions of doctrine, church organization and liturgical practices. The social status of membership also varied considerably among the denominations. As one might expect, each group laid claim to being the church most faithful to Scripture and true to Christian tradition. Not one but many churches were faced with the new world created by the Industrial Revolution, and the reasons for such a multiplicity of sects can be found in the long history of English Christianity.

Evidences of Christianity can be found as early as Roman Britain around 300 A.D. (Legend has it that Joseph of Arimathea had visited Britain in the first century bringing with him the Holy Grail or cup used at the Last Supper.) When Rome withdrew her legions, native Christians were driven into the fringes of the British Isles by pagan, Germanic invaders--Angles, Saxons and Danes. After Pope Gregory I sent the missionary Augustine to found a church in Kent in 597 A.D., Christianity experienced a steady recovery.

Throughout medieval times, English Christians were part of the Roman Catholic Church. Like Christianity elsewhere in Europe, English Catholicism was often troubled by heresy and by disagreements between ecclesiastical and secular authorities over money and legal jurisdiction. The most celebrated of such events in England was the bitter quarrel between Henry II, the most powerful of medieval princes, and Thomas Becket, Archbishop of Canterbury. The strife between these one-time friends resulted in Becket's murder in his cathedral at Canterbury on December 29, 1170.

Although disagreements did exist between the English Church and Rome at the beginning of the sixteenth century, most English Catholics were loyal to the papacy. King Henry VIII (1509-1547) even produced an anti-Lutheran pamphlet, Defense of the Seven Sacraments. For this welcome service during the time of Reformation troubles, Pope Leo X awarded him the title, Defender of the Faith. Such harmony was not to continue for very long. Out of a variety of motives--love for Anne Boleyn, his desperate search for a male heir, perhaps even a bad conscience--Henry VIII, with

the cooperation of his Parliaments, broke with Rome in 1533.
Henry declared himself to be the head of the English or Anglican
Church. Catholic monasteries were soon dissolved and their lands
sold, the profits going into the royal treasury. Although Henry
had no sympathy with Protestant beliefs, such doctrines as justification by faith and the reliance on Scripture over tradition
did begin to appear in England well before his reign ended in 1547.

The middle years of the sixteenth century found England torn
by religious strife. Protestant "heretics" like Thomas Cranmer,
Archbishop of Canterbury for twenty years, suffered death at the
stake in 1556 during "Bloody" Mary Tudor's campaign to reinstate
Catholicism. When Henry's daughter by Anne Boleyn, Elizabeth,
ascended to the throne in 1558, the religious issue was the greatest source of political and social instability.

Measured by its cultural expression the Elizabethan Age was a
glorious time when literature, art, music and theatre all flourishe
Yet, society seethed with religious bitterness through which Elizabeth and her chief counselors wisely pursued a middle course. The
open practice of Catholicism was prohibited and those who wished to
purify (hence the name Puritan) the Anglican Church of the vestiges
of Catholicism were also persecuted. Elizabeth's methods were
harsh but she did gain a religious settlement which temporarily
appeased the majority of her subjects.

She remained the supreme governor (the term "head" was no
longer used out of deference to Catholics who could consider none
but the Pope as head of the Church) of the Anglican Church. A
summary of Anglican doctrines known as the Thirty-Nine Articles
was adopted and Parliament further specified that all Christian
worship should follow the prescribed liturgies in the Book of
Common Prayer. Although it was clearly Protestant in terms of
beliefs, the structure of the Church of England and forms of worship did retain much of the Catholic heritage. Elizabeth's
strategy was a success. When she died, people mourned her as they
had not done for any other monarch of her turbulent century.

Elizabeth's successors, her Stuart cousins, were by no means
so fortunate. James I (1603-1625) brought an inflated view of his
own power to the English throne which antagonized members of
Parliament. During Elizabeth's time they had become accustomed
to playing a significant role in the determination of public
affairs. The reign of James I was the scene of many a bitter
debate; but it was his son, Charles I (1625-1649), who bore the
terrible consequences.

Charles I and his advisors were of the opinion that the king, not Parliament, was the supreme authority in the realm. The power to tax without Parliament's consent was asserted. It was also maintained that the Anglican clergy, from the Archbishop of Canterbury down to the parish priest, was the chief buttress of royal authority. Puritanism, rebelling against the worldliness and the episcopal structure of the Anglican Church, had grown strong, and was especially prevalent among the small landowners, lesser gentry and commercial classes. The degree to which their hostility to Charles I was motivated either by religious grievances or economic frustration has been a much discussed historical question but there is no guessing at the outcome of their hatred.

The Civil War or Puritan Revolution erupted in 1642. After suffering initial defeats, the Parliamentary forces gained decisive victories over the king's men. Parliament's success was due in part to the outstanding military leadership of Oliver Cromwell. Charles was captured and in 1649 he was convicted of treason and beheaded. From 1649 to 1660, England became a republic, a commonwealth in which real power, however, lay in the hands of Oliver Cromwell and the Puritan army. During these years, the radical Puritans attempted to make England into a kingdom of saints. The Anglican Church was abolished; statues, fine wooden carvings and priceless stained-glass windows were smashed. Laws were passed against nearly all forms of amusement and vice such as horse racing and gambling. By the time of Cromwell's death in 1658, public dissatisfaction with such religious fanaticism led to a desire for more normal conditions.

Exiled Charles II was recalled in 1660. The Anglican Church was soon reestablished and worship again conducted according to the Book of Common Prayer. The religious pendulum moved far from the Puritan side. Those, who in good conscience could not conform, became known as Nonconformists or Dissenters. Against them and the remaining Catholics, Parliament passed several important bills, the Test and Corporation Acts. These laws made it extremely difficult for Dissenters and impossible for sincere Catholics to engage in any form of political activity or hold public office.

When Charles II, the "merry monarch", died in 1685 he was followed by his brother, James II (1685-1688), whose arrogance and pro-Catholic policies were a serious grievance to all Protestants. James was ejected from the land in the peaceful and Glorious Revolution of 1688 and his Protestant daughter, Mary with her Dutch husband, William of Orange, were called to be co-monarchs. In the legislation following the revolution, Parliament not only established its supremacy over the crown but it also passed an Act of Toleration. Complete religious freedom was not granted but it was now possible for Dissenters to worship openly without fear of persecution. Laws were maintained against Catholics but in the years following they were not enforced with much vigor. Dissenters were still denied the right to hold public office unless they "occasionally conformed" to Anglican worship and they were refused access to the Universities of Oxford and Cambridge. However these disabilities were really not of a serious nature.

The Dissenters were far from being united. A number of different groups--Presbyterians, Congregationalists, Baptists and Quakers--already existed. The Anglican Church too would soon experience division. To understand the nature of English Christianity during the early Victorian years, it is essential to appreciate fully eighteenth-century social developments. As we have seen, the Industrial Revolution had marked consequences throughout the Victorian age; of equal importance were the changes within the pre-Victorian Christian churches.

The Church of England

The Church of England was the church, established by law, for the people of England and Wales. Scotland had experienced its own reformation and, although Scotland, since 1707, was governed by the Parliament of Great Britain, the Scottish Presbyterian Church was completely independent. An established episcopal Church of Ireland also existed. Although Ireland too was directly governed from London after 1800, the vast majority of the inhabitants remained Roman Catholics.

In 1830, the Church of England was structured in much the same way as it had been for several centuries. The Crown remained the nominal governor of the Church but the actual work of Christian ministry was conducted by a vast and complicated bureaucracy. At the apex of this ecclesiastical pyramid stood the Archbishops of York and Canterbury, the latter having been recognized since medieval times as superior. Included in these two archdioceses were twenty-four dioceses, each presided over by a bishop. His task was to supervise the work of the vicar or parson in the local parish church. If the appointed vicar failed to reside in his parish as often happened the day to day ministry would be entrusted to a younger clergyman or curate. The bishops resided in palaces next to splendid cathedrals like Lincoln, Winchester or Exeter. Frequently the humble and poorly paid curate lived in a remote parish beside a crumbling old church. There was an enormous difference of wealth and power between bishop and priest.

Over the centuries the Church of England as a whole had grown wealthy. Pious Christians often endowed churches or included the church in their wills. The clergy were supported by profits from the lands attached to the churches. But these were not the only sources of ecclesiastical funds. Wealthy parishoners also rented the very pews in which they sat, providing revenue for the church and a status symbol for themselves. The poor either stood during services or sat on rough benches. Fees were collected for the clergyman's services at marriages, baptisms and burials. Everyone, even Dissenters and Catholics, had to pay taxes or rates in support of the established religion. Over the years, the structure of the Anglican Church, like the political system, had become antiquated and filled with abuse. In 1830, the Church stood in obvious need of reform and revitalization.

The Thirty-Nine Articles and the Book of Common Prayer only provided a framework in which a wide span of Christian activity might take place. At the beginning of the eighteenth century, the beliefs and practices of Anglicanism were affected by two important and related developments. Because of their distaste for religious or Puritan extremism, Anglican clergy and educated laity stood firmly against all forms of religious "enthusiasm". Sermons preached from Anglican pulpits became noted for their moderation. Religious zeal or emotionalism of any kind was abandoned to the extent that Communion was celebrated infrequently and the singing of hymns seldom practiced.

More importantly, the Oxford and Cambridge-educated clergy were of the opinion that human reason, cool and dispassionate, could provide an adequate basis for Christian belief. During the seventeenth century, England had been the center of important scientific and philosophical activity. The "natural philosophers", as the scientists were called, claimed that God was best comprehended by systematically delving into nature's mysteries. The most famous of all natural philosophers, Isaac Newton (1643-1727), believed that the natural laws which he wrote in complex mathematical symbols were God-given and were good. John Locke (1632-1704), who influenced thinking about psychology and politics for a century, wrote an essay in 1695 on the Reasonableness of Christianity. Although his ideas cast many traditional Christian doctrines such as original sin into doubt, Locke's attitude toward Christianity established a long-lasting pattern among the better educated members of society.

Deism--the belief that God's only function was that of a first cause--was not too widely held but neither was it condemned by the Anglican clergy during the Age of Reason. Near the end of the eighteenth century, William Paley (1743-1805), a Cambridge man and author of <u>Evidences of Christianity,</u> found wide acceptance for his analogy of God as a fine watchmaker. He claimed that the smoothly ticking universe testified, in a far better way than the Bible itself, that an intelligent and good supreme being was ultimately responsible.

In such an intellectual milieu, theologians, the parish clergy and the laymen who could understand, concluded that God was not very adequately revealed by the scientifically doubtful tales contained in Scripture; and they were convinced that he was certainly not revealed directly by mystical or emotional experiences. This was sterile theology and unlively religion removing God far from the day to day lives of mortals. Hand in hand with such rational theology was the feeling that God expected no extraordinary behavior from his creatures; He did not desire perfection but only that people deal honestly and reasonably with each other.

Eighteenth-century Englishmen, from lords to laborers, were not especially known for their piety or learning. It was not perhaps altogether bad that they should receive a weekly admonition to behave themselves; a well-educated and conscientious parson might indeed raise the general level of culture among his parishioners. But the Church of England was soon proved to lack the major ingredient of any vital religious institution. It had no spirit. Although a considerable element of dryness would remain until Victoria's day, great changes were already in the making.

John Wesley and the Evangelical Revival

The whirlwind of religious change which swept over England in the eighteenth century (America too was deeply affected) spirals down to the person of John Wesley (1703-1791). John and his brother Charles (1707-1788) were born to a family which had produced many clergymen. In 1720, Wesley entered Oxford University, his heart set on becoming a minister. Following his ordination, Wesley assisted his father but, in 1729, Wesley returned to Oxford as a fellow of Lincoln College. Together with several other scholars, John and Charles Wesley formed a group known as the Holy Club. This was hardly a popular fraternity among the unruly young gentlemen of Oxford. Wesley and his friends were derisively called

"Methodists" because they so strictly observed religious duties. The club conducted regular devotions, Bible study, fasts and charitable work among the Oxford poor.

Wesley's career took an abrupt turn in 1735 when he left England, at the invitation of Governor James Ogelthorpe, to minister in the colony of Georgia. There he was impressed with the spirit of Moravian immigrants--pious German people who sought to create exemplary Christian communities. The people of Georgia, however, were generally unimpressed with Wesley and, in 1737, he returned to England.

On May 24, 1738, Wesley experienced an altogether new sense of Christian conviction. His Journal contains this report about a meeting he attended at a London Moravian society:

> In the evening, I went very unwillingly to a society in Aldersgate Street, where one was reading Luther's preface to the Epistle to the Romans. About a quarter to nine, while he was describing the change which God works in the heart through faith in Christ, I felt my heart strangely warmed. I felt that I did trust in Christ, Christ alone, for salvation; and an assurance was given me that he had taken away my sins, even mine and saved me from the law of sin and death.

From that time until his death, John Wesley lived as a man possessed by a righteous spirit. His mission was to kindle a vital spirit of Christianity in the hearts of all who would hear him.

Wesley had no parish church of his own and, because of his "enthusiasm", he found that Anglican clergy were not anxious to have him as a visitor in their pulpits. His friend, George Whitefield (1714-1770), who was to become a great preacher in both England and America, suggested that they preach to the poor and unchurched in the fields and city streets. Wesley was a conservative when it came to ecclesiastical custom and, at first, he objected to the idea but Whitefield convinced him that it was the only way to take the Gospel to the people.

The remainder of Wesley's life is a story of action. Starting in 1739, he tramped the British Isles, eventually traveling over a quarter of a million miles. He preached between forty and fifty thousand sermons. At times he was roughly handled by antagonistic crowds but more often people came, especially the poor, to listen attentively. Many instances have been recorded of people having exceptional religious experiences during Wesley's powerful sermons. He emphasized the reality of human sin and the necessity of repentance; he spoke eloquently of the redemptive work of Jesus, God's grace and the necessity for personal reformation leading to a life of disciplined devotion to God and service to mankind. Unlike the dreary Anglicans, Wesley urged the use of extemporary prayer and encouraged the singing of hymns, many of which were written by his brother, Charles.

Of the thousands who were attracted to Methodism, many came from the Church of England and from Dissenting Churches. But from rural England and the early factory towns, came people who had been bypassed by the other Christian churches and who found a need for personal and spiritual fulfillment satisfied.

John Wesley was more than an itinerant revivalist. He was an organizer without peer. In each locality he visited, Wesley left behind a Methodist society, a group which would meet weekly for prayer, study and mutual admonition. The spiritual welfare of each member was the immediate concern of all others and each was also expected to participate actively. Some had responsibility for collecting funds to meet the society's expenses; others became readers. The especially gifted among the laymen were even asked into the pulpit.

Wesley organized these societies into a "Connexion". Although this was not a distinct denomination because Wesley never wanted to be separated from the Church of England, the inevitable break did come in 1784 when he consented to ordain Methodist ministers for service in British colonies. After his death, a constitution for the Methodists was established placing governing power in the hands of an annual Conference composed of traveling Methodist preachers.

The emphases on personal religion, scripture study, conversion and a life of piety and mission--collectively termed Evangelicalism were not restricted to the Methodists. It is correct to see John Wesley as the leading figure in the great religious or evangelical revival taking place in the second half of the eighteenth century. Members of the Church of England and of the Dissenting congregation forsook the sterile rationalism of orthodoxy theology to follow a more spiritual religion. At times their religiosity could degenerate to mere emotionalism and their piety was not untinged with snobbishness. Despite these shortcomings, the Evangelical revival was the most significant movement in Christianity since the Reformation, finding a social outlet in a variety of worthy causes.

Like Wesley, most evangelicals were conservative politically, seeking to change the human heart rather than the social system. They did, however, accomplish considerable public good. Evangelicals worked for an improvement in the moral standards of British society by condemning the brutality and the sexual permissiveness, both so characteristic of the eighteenth century. Temperance societies and schools for the poor were founded; orphanages and houses for "fallen" women were constructed. They also protested against the grosser evils, especially child labor, to be found in the early factory system.

One group of wealthy evangelicals within the Church of England was centered in the London suburb of Clapham. Not only did they stress personal piety but public work as well. The most famous member of this group was William Wilberforce (1759-1833), the greatest Parliamentary orator of his day. He mounted a campaign against the slave trade and, in 1807, it was abolished. When slavery in the British colonies was completely abolished in 1833 Evangelical Christians could take a large measure of credit.

The impact of the Evangelical revival on the early Victorians must not be underestimated. Children of middle class parents grew up in an atmosphere of earnest religiosity in which Bible reading and prayers filled many hours each week. From infancy many Victorians were conditioned to a life of Christian duty and discipline. The problem was, of course, that the Evangelical spirit was so easily perverted into rigid formalism and narrow-minded ideas concerning respectability.

Evangelicals were noted for their concern with Biblical knowledge and personal conversion. Those early Victorian Christians who emphasized strict adherence to ecclesiastical traditions and who kept denominational differences clearly in mind became designated as "High Church". Those who desired, on the other hand, interdenominational cooperation and who were willing to overlook doctrinal differences were termed "Broad Church". For all-- Evangelicals, High and Broad Church--the common denominator was the seriousness with which they took their Christianity. Such earnestness would lead these Christians to explore many different paths within the framework of Victorian society.

27

Dissenters

The initial fires of Dissent had cooled considerably during
the eighteenth century. The Act of Toleration which allowed
Dissenters the freedom of worship deprived them of a precious
grievance. Some eventually returned to the Church of England
for social reasons. Like the Anglicans, certain Dissenting sects
were deeply influenced by rationalism and some by the Evangelical revival. Members of Dissenting congregations generally
prospered economically during the eighteenth century with many
of the leading figures of the Industrial Revolution associated
with Dissent. The academies which Dissenters founded because
they were not allowed to attend the universities were excellent
schools, providing an education often superior to that of Oxford
and Cambridge.

In 1828, the political status of Dissenters was clarified
when Parliament finally repealed the Test and Corporation Acts.
These laws had become virtual dead letters. Now Dissenters were
completely free to participate in British political life. However they still had to pay taxes to support the Church of England,
to be married by an Anglican clergyman, and were excluded from
Oxford and Cambridge until mid-century. The repeal of the Test
and Corporation Acts indicates, of course, that Dissent was no
longer seen as a threat to political order. It also provides an
opportunity to examine the differences among the major Dissenting
denominations.

Methodists

The story of organized Methodism from the death of Wesley to
the mid-nineteenth century is one of rapid growth on the one hand
and extreme division in the ranks on the other. Beginning the
century with less than 100,000 members, the Wesleyan Methodists
reached 360,000 by 1850. Rapid population growth coupled with the
fact that the Church of England simply did not have enough seats
in its churches to accommodate the people must be given some
responsibility for the dramatic increase. But there is no denying
the clear fact that for many people, especially those who found
their lives uprooted by industrialization, the Methodist society

provided a sense of community and of individual worth.[1]

Decision making authority in the Methodist church after Wesley's death lay with the Conference of traveling preachers, all of whom had been personally appointed by Wesley. Naturally they retained the conservative positions of their master. For all his appeal to the poor and ill-educated, Wesley had been distinctly "High Church" in terms of governance. Only ordained clergy should make decisions. Shortly before his death, Wesley had made his ideas on lay participation in the governance of Methodism unmistakeably clear:

> As long as I live, the people shall have no share in choosing either stewards or leaders among the Methodists. We have not, and never had, any such customs. We are no republicans, and never intend to be.

No one agreed more strongly than the Rev. Jabez Bunting (1779-1858) who earned the title of "Methodist Pope" in the first part of the nineteenth century.

A good many Methodists, accustomed as they had become to active participation and the services of lay preachers, were not content with such an authoritarian structure. An early illustration of dissatisfaction was provided in 1797 when a small group, calling themselves the Methodist "New Connexion", was formed because they advocated camp meetings and lay representation at the annual Conference. The majority of the Methodist clergy was dead set against such propositions. The leader of the New Connexion was Alexander Kilham (1762-98). (New Connexion Methodists were often called Kilhamites.) Of far more significance were the Primitive Methodists who split from the Wesleyans in 1810. By mid-century they could claim a membership of 100,000 and well over twice that many people could usually be found worshipping with the Primitive Methodists.

---

[1]The brilliant French historian Elie Halevy, History of the English People in the Nineteenth Century (1913) believed that the theology and structure of Methodism were responsible for short-circuiting revolutionary fervor among the working classes. This challenging thesis has stirred more than its share of controversy. See the comments of E.J. Hobsbawm, Labouring Men (1964).

The Primitive Methodists respected their Wesleyan heritage but believed the rigidity of men like Jabez Bunting constituted a departure from the early spirit of Methodism. They began as street revivalists, referred to as "Ranters" by those who thought their methods crude. The people attracted to Primitive Methodism were often of a comparatively low economic and social level. Wesleyan Methodist chapels may have been frequented by shop foremen and tradesmen but it was the factory worker and plain-speaking miner together with their wives and children who attended a Primitive Methodist meeting.

Primitive Methodists did not condemn political action as did the strict Wesleyans. Chartists, who often had little use for organized Christianity, were frequently to be found in their chapels. Primitive Methodists were also concerned with eliminating social evils, especially the use of alcohol. The excessive use and unregulated selling of alcohol was surely one of the most vicious social consequences of the Industrial Revolution. The word "teetotal" was given to the language by the Primitive Methodists who stood so solidly behind total abstention that they used unfermented juice in place of wine at their communion services. But the Primitives were also the victims of their success. By the 1840s they too had become over-regulated by their annual Conference and had increasingly left the streets for the more socially respectable chapel.

Presbyterians, Unitarians and Congregationalists

Of all Dissenting groups the Methodists had become the most numerous. The other denominations could trace a heritage going back beyond Wesley to seventeenth-century Puritanism. For the older Dissenting congregations, the eighteenth century had been a moribund period. Numbering at least 300,000 at the beginning, they declined in both numbers and spirit.

The largest group of old Dissenters had been the Presbyterians who, as their name implies, stood opposed to the episcopal structur of the restored Anglican Church. During the course of the eighteen century, English Presbyterianism virtually disappeared.[2] Under the

---

[2]English Presbyterians did exist during the Victorian age but they sprang from Scottish influence rather than from English Puritanism.

influence of rationalism, many Presbyterians became Unitarian. The Bible did remain their guide but they came to believe that the doctrine of the Trinity was not to be found in Scripture. Others went a step further and denied the validity of Scripture because it did not always conform to reason. Although the Unitarians were not a large body, they did include some very notable people.

The leading figure in Unitarianism of the late eighteenth century had been Joseph Priestley (1733-1804), a man of many and extraordinary talents. Known chiefly for the discovery of oxygen in 1774, Priestley wrote widely on political topics as well as science. He believed in individualism and popular government; by expressing sympathy with the French Revolution, Priestley so angered the public that his Birmingham home and laboratory were destroyed by a mob. In 1793 he emigrated to the United States. Priestley had begun his career as a Presbyterian minister. However, his theology was too radical for his congregation; he did not accept the doctrine of the atonement, and he denied the divine inspiration of the Scriptures and the literal truth of the Bible. Nevertheless, Priestley was a very religious man, believing in the eternal existence of God and the necessity for high moral standards.

Following Priestley's intellectual orientation to theology, Presbyterian-Unitarian clergymen became increasingly able to reach only the minds of the very well-educated. In the nineteenth century, English Unitarians would begin to incorporate features of the Evangelical revival. The man chiefly responsible was the Unitarian minister and philosopher, James Martineau (1805-1900).[3] Although Martineau revitalized Unitarian liturgy and used such features as Wesleyan hymns, the Unitarians always remained an isolated denomination because other Victorian Christians always doubted whether a Unitarian could be correctly classified as a Christian.

The Congregationalists or Independents were another of the old Dissenting groups. Believing that each individual congregation of Christians was absolutely supreme, all forms of federation were refused until the Congregational Union was formed in 1831. The Congregationalists numbered perhaps one-half million souls in their

---

[3] His sister was Harriet Martineau (1802-1876), one of the most brilliant and renowned of Victorian women.

chapels and were served by well-trained clergymen. In terms of their Protestant beliefs, Congregationalists were the heirs of Calvinism emphasizing that God's grace was delivered only to His elect. Very similar to the Congregationalists were the Baptists, differing only in their belief that infants should not be baptized. The major distinction was in social composition; Congregationalists were thoroughly middle class people while the Baptists attracted more laborers.

Quakers

The Quakers or Society of Friends occupied a strange position in early Victorian society. Founded by George Fox (1624-1691), the Quakers sprang from the most radical religious groups thrown up by the Puritan Revolution. Recognizing no authority but God's immediate revelation (inner light) the Quakers made a serious attempt to cut themselves off from all worldliness. They dressed simply, used "thee" and "thou", and took Scripture so literally that they would neither give legal oaths nor accept military service. Much persecuted during the Restoration period, many emigrated to America when William Penn was granted a charter for the Quaker colony of Pennsylvania in 1681.

In Victoria's day they were respected rather than ridiculed for their beliefs. Although the Quakers were never numerous--numbering approximately 15,000 during the Victorian era--they exercised considerable influence. For example, Quakers had worked hard in the campaign to abolish slavery in the British colonies. A number of important Victorian politicians came from Quaker families, the most noteworthy being John Bright (1811-1889) who led the fight to repeal the Corn Laws.

Catholics

In 1800 only about 1% of the English were Roman Catholics. By 1850, their numbers would have greatly increased as a result of the immigration of large numbers of Irish. The horrors of famine and the injustice of the landlord-tenant system in Ireland drove Irish Catholics by the millions to England and to America.

The first significant event for English Roman Catholics in the nineteenth century was their political emancipation. This important act of Parliament was not the product of pressure from the small Catholic community in England but resulted from the agitation of Irish politicians. Led by Daniel O'Connell (1775-1847), Irish leaders, hoping eventually for complete Home Rule, brought a good deal of pressure on the Tory government. The Emancipation Bill became law in 1829. Provided they had sufficient income, Catholics in England and Ireland could now vote and could even sit in Parliament if they swore an oath not to do anything which would undermine the Protestant religion. It would not, however, be in the arena of politics that English Catholics would make the most news. Even as Victoria was coming to the throne, respected and high ranking Anglican churchmen were asking if Roman Catholic beliefs and traditions might not indeed be compatible with Anglicanism.

Millennialists and Freethinkers

Millennialists believe that the Second Coming of Christ will lead to the establishment of a new Kingdom, one which will last for a thousand years. Suffering will be brought to an end; all which is wrong with the world will be made right; the righteous will rule with Christ. Although millennialists disagree over the precise time and style of the Second Coming, they are united in their expectation of dramatic change. Such groups flourished during the late eighteenth and early nineteenth centuries, nourished by industrialization itself which led them to expect even more rapid changes in the future. The Evangelical revival, by placing so much emphasis on Bible study, served to acquaint many people with the apocalyptic passages of the book of Revelations. Millennialism may also have been a means of psychological escape from economic oppression.

The English millennial sects were always linked to a prophet-figure, a man or woman claiming to speak for or actually to be the new messiah. One was Edward Irving (1792-1834), a former Presbyterian, who established a large London following in the 1820s. His meetings were often characterized by speaking in tongues and other charismatic manifestations. Some millennialists, Ann Lee (1736-1784) of Manchester who founded the Shakers for example, emigrated to America where millennial movements flourished in the frontier environment. Such prophets sometimes came to a tragic end; one self-proclaimed messiah and his followers clashed with the police in Kent in 1838 and were killed. Although these groups had died out by the 1850s, they did articulate the desperation of the working classes. It is significant that the socialist,

33

Robert Owen, adopted millennialist rhetoric in proclaiming his secular version of the new moral world.

At the opposite end of the religious spectrum were the anti-Christian freethinkers or atheists as they called themselves. Like the millennialists they attracted notoriety and hostility far beyond their numerical strength. In many little newssheets and scattered meeting halls around Britain these heirs of eighteenth century radicalism condemned Christianity. Their attacks were not directed so much against Christian beliefs as against the churches and the clergy for failing to live up to their own standards of Christian conduct.

Victorian law was definitely not on the side of the outspoken freethinker. Richard Carlile (1790-1843), was imprisoned during the 1820's for publishing the radical works of Tom Paine. George Jacob Holyoake (1817-1906), who later helped organize the Secular Society, was jailed in 1842 on charges of blasphemy, still a punishable offense in the early Victorian years. Free thought did attract a few intellectuals and some workingmen but it never became a popular movement. Churchmen, however, were alerted by "atheist missionaries" to what they saw as a growing problem, the infidelity of the working classes.

Despite the pronounced religiosity of the British during the first half of the nineteenth century it was increasingly apparent that working class families were being reached neither by Anglicans nor by Dissenters. For one thing there were simply not enough churches to serve the needs of the expanded urban population. But even new city churches were never full. What would be the moral, social and political consequences of the apparent decline in religiosity? Pious Victorians shuddered to think. The evidence which confirmed their alarming suspicions came from one of the most famous public documents of the Victorian era.

The Religious Census

On 30 March 1851, clergymen of all denominations, as part of the national census, were required to record attendance at Sunday morning, afternoon and evening services. The purpose was to provide a general picture of religious observance. At the end of a two-year period of intensive study of the vast amount of information, a report was compiled and presented to Parliament. Althoug portions of the analysis were called into question there is every reason to believe that this report was highly accurate. The total population for England and Wales stood at 17,927,609 according to the national census with church attendance as follows:

Church Attendance -- March 30, 1851

```
Church of England. . . . . . . . . 5,292,551
Roman Catholic . . . . . . . . . .   383,630
Dissenters (combined). . . . . . 4,536,264
```

The religious census made allowance for the fact that some people certainly attended church more than once on that Sunday and took into consideration that many people--the sick, the very young and old, or those in necessary occupations--could not attend church.

But the statistics were shocking. First of all, it appeared that the Church of England no longer could claim a commanding majority of the nation's church members. Roughly 52% of those attending services did so in an Anglican church. Why then, Dissenters asked, should the Church of England still continue to enjoy such special status? Another disconcerting figure was the surprisingly large number of Roman Catholics who were now to be found in England.

The figure which caused most worry for Anglicans and Dissenters alike was that of the five million or so people who were apparently able but for some reason chose not to attend any church. By twentieth century standards, these Victorians worshipped in massive numbers. By their own standards it seemed that something dreadful had taken place. Could it be that millions of people no longer even made an effort to worship God? There was little doubt as to which sector of society the non-worshippers belonged. The middle classes and the rural people were still in church; the working classes were staying home.

In 1851, Victorian Christians had, for several decades, been in the process of coming to grips with serious intellectual and social issues. It is to that story that we first must turn. Other problems were still beyond their horizons. As many clergymen or concerned laymen pondered the Religious Census, one fact seemed to be very clear: the modern age had ushered in more than industrial changes. Beliefs and values--the components of the human con-science--were becoming secularized.

CHAPTER III.   THE CHURCH IN THE EARLY VICTORIAN AGE

Politics and the Church of England

Whigs and Tories both were given the opportunity to govern the realm between the enactment of the Great Reform Bill and the repeal of the Corn Laws in 1846. The ministry which held power in 1832, headed by the elderly Earl Grey (1764-1845), was composed of moderate Whigs. Because of their fear that radical elements within the Whig party would push for further unsavory measures, the Tories generally lent their support to Grey's ministry. In the summer of 1834, Grey retired and his office was taken by Viscount Melbourne (1779-1848) who headed the government until 1841, with the exception of several months in early 1835 when Sir Robert Peel (1788-1850) and the Tories were in office.

Melbourne was a cynical man, aristocratic, vain and with little sense of the real problems of the country. He did, however, possess a considerable talent for managing political factions and personalities. Although it is somewhat surprising that such a man could capture the loyalty of the young Queen, Victoria grew deeply attached to Melbourne, so much so that she nearly created a constitutional crisis in 1839. When she was forced to call upon Peel to form a ministry because Melbourne believed his own political position too weak to continue as Prime Minister, Victoria insisted on retaining her Whig ladies-in-waiting. Sensing the queen's hostility and not really wanting to accept the reins of government quite yet, Peel refused to form a cabinet. Thus, the Whig administration was forced to continue for another two years. The considerable amount of legislation--the new Poor Law, Factory Acts, Municipal Reform--which had been passed during these years created enemies for the Whigs. They began to find themselves divided and increasingly unpopular in the country.

Peel finally took the office of Prime Minister in 1841. Even though he had been out of office during most of the 1830s, Peel was the most respected politician of the age, recognized by all as a man of principle, talent and great administrative experience. Compared to the fatherly Melbourne, Peel was thought a "cold, odd man" by Victoria. Nevertheless she soon came to believe that Tory conservatism was far preferable to Whiggism.

The 1840s were the most difficult years of the nineteenth century; unemployment was high, the Chartists continued to agitate for further parliamentary reform and one of history's most terrible famines swept Ireland. Similar economic conditions in Europe propelled nations toward the revolutionary days of 1848. It is in large part due to Peel's statesmanship, putting policy above party interests, that Britain weathered the hungry forties in comparative political tranquility. Peel's greatest triumph, the repeal of the Corn Laws, also brought his political downfall. Angry that their leader should have abandoned agricultural interests, a large faction of disgusted Tories combined with the Whigs to defeat him. Peel's belief that food should be more freely imported and his desire to alleviate the plight of the Irish destroyed the old Tory party. Until his death in 1850, caused by a fall from his horse, Sir Robert Peel remained a central figure in politics. In the words of one leading historian of the Victorian age, the 1840s was Peel's decade.[1]

Peel's wide interests had included far more than agricultural tariff reform. In 1829 he had played a significant part in bringing about Catholic emancipation. An ardent supporter of the Church of England, Peel decided to work for much needed reform measures. In 1834 he had outlined to his constituents in Tamworth the measures of ecclesiastical reform to be achieved. He believed that Dissenters should be relieved of their remaining disabilities--payment of church rates and the requirement to be married only by an Anglican clergyman. Although his Tamworth Manifesto was condemned by his political foes as mere opportunism, Peel proved that he was true to his word.

Reform for the Church of England was more than a purely religious issue. It was intertwined with Dissenting grievances and with the liberal belief that all citizens should be treated equally before the law. On the other hand, the entrenched social power of the Church of England could hardly be taken lightly. Here was a cause guaranteed to produce political headaches.

Doctrines and forms of worship had been significantly modified by the Reformation and the Evangelical Revival of the eighteenth century. However, the ecclesiastical apparatus which had

---

[1]R.K. Webb, _Modern England_ (New York, 1968).

weathered the impact of seventeenth century Puritanism, was almost medieval. Several centuries of administrative neglect had made matters worse. The sins were age-old ecclesiastical ones. First was pluralism--one clergyman serving in more than one assignment and therefore receiving multiple incomes.[2] Pluralism often was a necessity because small parishes did not have enough income to provide a parson with an adequate living. Because clergymen were certainly not immune to the enticements of wealth, there were also many cases of men deriving income of thousands of pounds per year and doing little or nothing in return.

A related problem was the distribution of wealth. Bishops might have incomes of thousands of pounds, in some cases of over Ł100,000 per year. Deans and canons attached to well-endowed cathedrals were handsomely rewarded while a lowly curate might be required to scrape by on as little as Ł80, supplementing his income by farming or tutoring local boys. In 1831, the radical journalist, John Wade, published a muckracking volume entitled the Extra-ordinary Black Book in which he listed the hefty incomes of the bishops. His message was not unheeded when he condemned the Church of England and Ireland for being the most unreformed church in all Christendom.[3]

Compared to pluralism and inordinate income differences among the clergy, the status of Dissenters was a less serious issue. Since the repeal of the Test and Corporation Acts, Dissenters had not been pressing too hard for their remaining disabilities to be eliminated. The situation was much different in Ireland.

The impoverished Irish Catholic peasants were required to render an annual tithe, an assessment on their meagre farm produce, taken by the Church of Ireland to maintain a top-heavy Protestant hierarchy of four Irish archbishops and eighteen bishops. In

---

[2] In 1827 less than half the Anglican clergy was found to be actually residing in the parishes they served.

[3] Although it had a separate ecclesiastical structure, the Church of Ireland was regarded as the Protestant, Anglican estab-lishment. It stood in the same relationship to Parliament as the Church of England.

reality these officials only served the Protestant minority. So much did the Irish Catholics resent this church tax that the British army had to be used on a number of occasions during the 1830s to keep peace at sites where cattle were being sold to raise the required tithe. Violence and even death were not uncommon.

This deplorable state of ecclesiastical affairs had pricked few political consciences during the comfortable eighteenth century, but in the nineteenth century a good many Victorians were insisting that all institutions be structured reasonably and efficiently. The Church of England fell far short of meeting acceptable standards. The problem, as with the reform of Parliament, was to divine some measure of change without initiating a period of destructive puritanism.

Political radicals and some Dissenters did desire to see the legal privileges of the Church of England completely swept away. A few radicals called for the separation of church and state along the lines of the American scheme. Propagandists for such drastic measures accomplished little except to stir up the public and to frighten the more fainthearted among the Anglican clergy who worried that their livings were soon to be disrupted and that they would find themselves turned into the streets.

Public opinion had certainly not been made more favorable to the Church by the behavior of the Anglican bishops in the House of Lords who had opposed the Reform Bill of 1832. Villified by radical pamphleteers, castigated as enemies of the people and alienated from the Whigs, churchmen feared that reform could lead only to the destruction of the ancient privileges of the Church.

Such fears were ultimately proved groundless. The Whigs did introduce legislation in early 1833 to reduce the size of the hierarchy in Ireland. Two archbishops and eight bishops were to have their offices eliminated. The part of this otherwise reasonable measure, known as the Church Temporalities Bill, which most horrified conservative clergymen was a clause requiring the funds, formerly allocated to these abolished positions, to be "applied to such purposes as Parliament shall hereafter appoint and decide". This clause was denounced from many an Anglican pulpit as robbery. In order to get a Parliamentary majority for the bill, the clause in question was withdrawn. Yet there was no rejoicing among conservative ecclesiastics.

During his short term as Prime Minister from January to April, 1835, Sir Robert Peel seized the initiative and began the most important phase of church reform. Peel was a devout Christian who believed in the necessity of reform; he also realized that change would be best undertaken if the necessary measures were presented by the Church of England rather than being imposed by politicians. Therefore he created a special Ecclesiastical Commission, composed of laymen and clergymen, to study church affairs thoroughly and to propose reforms to Parliament for approval. The Archbishop of Canterbury, William Howley (1766-1848), gave his blessing to the commission but the really energetic member was the Bishop of London, C.J. Bloomfield (1786-1857).

Whenever an investigation of national significance was conducted under the auspices of Parliament, commissions were created and they usually dragged their proceedings on for many months before reporting. This one was different. Peel placed himself on the commission and he, together with Bloomfield, saw to it that the first report was rendered in March, 1835. It called for the incomes of bishops to be roughly equalized and for some diocesan boundaries to be altered to reflect population shifts.

Less than one month later, Peel lost his majority in the Commons and had to resign. Melbourne, whose own religious beliefs were decidedly shallow, and the Whigs came back for another six years. But the Ecclesiastical Commission had begun to change the entire structure of the church. Melbourne renewed it and the commission continued its work, its recommendations to Parliament realized in a series of acts from 1836 to 1840. In addition to leveling the income of bishops, the number of positions held by a single clergyman was limited to two. About £350,000 per year were turned from the heavily endowed cathedrals over to the assistance of the poorer clergy and the most heavily populated parishes. Finally, the Ecclesiastical Commission successfully petitioned to be made a permanently functioning body.

Like the political and social legislation in early Victorian England, these ecclesiastical reforms were of a conservative nature. Gross abuses were reduced while the basic structure was retained intact. Just as political reform did not immediately create a government more responsive to the nation's needs, the church reforms did not, in themselves, result in a more conscientious clergy or an elevated religiosity among the public. Without such steps having been taken, however, popular discontent with the religious establishment would have become much greater and the eventual changes more drastic. The level of hostility to religious institutions, which was so pronounced in the continental nations during the nineteenth century, never was reached in Victorian England. The Church of England continued to exercise a profound impact on the ideas and ethics of the nation, especially among the Victorian middle classes.

These attempts to reform the Church of England, as well-meaning as they were, did bring unintended consequences. Many Anglican clergymen looked with horror at both Dissent and Liberalism, twin evils which were seen to be dominant elements within Parliament. Ever since the restoration of the monarchy in 1660, the Church of England had looked for its protection to the government. Perhaps the time had come when the political influence of the bishops was nearly gone. Was it not time to proclaim again that the authority of the Church within the world ultimately lay in its possession of the Biblical injunction to preach and to remit sin? Stronger reliance on Christian traditions, the mysteries of faith and liturgical arts might prove more effective in restoring the authority of the Church than by trying to defend its constitutional position.

In the Age of Reason, such sentiments would have provoked scorn for being "high church", too tinged with Roman Catholicism. By the early Victorian age, however, Englishmen and all other Europeans were experiencing that remarkable development which exalted rather than despised faith, tradition and beauty: Romanticism.

Romanticism and Samuel Taylor Coleridge

Like many other "isms", Romanticism is a term coined by scholars to encompass a wide range of associated activities. It was in France and in Germany during the end of the eighteenth and early nineteenth centuries where young intellectuals came to revolt most ardently against rationalism and the classical artistic standards of the Enlightenment. Poets and artists turned again to nature for congenial themes, searching either for pastoral simplicity and purity or rugged wilderness freedom. These characteristics, they judged, were absent from society.

The political and social ideas adopted by Romantics also covered a broad spectrum. Some sought a return to monarchical despotism; others followed the notions of Jean Jacques Rousseau

and his interpreters to become revolutionary advocates of that
absolute freedom which the human race was presumed to have enjoyed
in its infancy before being corrupted by society and government.
Whether in politics or the arts, the activities of the Romantics
have been so diverse as to defy the easy generalization. The
common thread, however, is their rejection of the Enlightenment
conviction that reason alone could achieve progress.

The extreme political views associated with Romanticism were
only occasionally to be found in Britain. But English poets,
artists and writers did more than join in rejecting their eighteenth century heritage; they helped to lead the revolt. William
Blake (1757-1827) could claim a multitude of followers for his
conviction that the inner vision of truth was superior to objec-
tive reality. The middle ages, the age of faith rather than
science, was no longer thought a time of darkness and ridiculous
superstition but as an age in which people had arrived at higher
levels of truth. The novels of Sir Walter Scott (1771-1832)
popularized the medieval virtues. William Wordsworth (1770-1850)
hymned the beauties of nature in contrast to the ugliness of
industrial society and the sterility of book learning. It was a
time of great landscape painting by John Constable (1776-1837)
and J.W. Turner (1775-1851). Architects, like Sir Charles Barry
(1795-1837) who designed the present Houses of Parliament, gave
fresh appreciation to the long despised Gothic styles.

It is hardly possible to single out an individual who dominated the English Romantic movement, but there was one--the
greatest genius of them all--whose work had profound significance
not only for literature but also for Christianity during the
Victorian age: Samuel Taylor Coleridge (1772-1834). He was the
most important British apologist for Christian belief in the
Romantic era. Yet Coleridge was a layman, his only direct link
to the Church of England being that he was the last of fourteen
children born to a Devonshire parson.

As a child, Coleridge gave evidence of a precocious mind. He
never completed his university degree, although he was a distinguished student at Cambridge. In spite of his talents, Coleridge's
personal life was a shambles; his health was poor and for years he
was addicted to opium. Brilliant, his existence an agony,
Coleridge produced volumes of poetry and essays. His fame was
guaranteed as early as 1789 when he cooperated with Wordsworth in
producing the Lyrical Ballads which contained his Rime of the
Ancient Mariner. No less a figure in the history of ideas than

43

John Stuart Mill thought Coleridge to be one of the two seminal minds of the early nineteenth century; Bentham was Mill's other selection.

On a generation of young people, many of whom were tired of old religious formulas, Coleridge proved to have great influence. His widely read <u>Aids to Reflection,</u> published in 1825, defined Christianity as "not a theory, or a speculation; but a life--not a philosophy of life, but a life and a living process." There need be no fear in seeking after truth, claimed Coleridge, for the foundation of Christianity did not lie in rationally derived propositions but in the depths of the human conscience. Dogma, even the Scriptures, were of secondary importance.

Coleridge's theological views seemed extremely unorthodox to many churchmen. They were. But Coleridge also defended the Church of England. He believed the church should be all-inclusive, achieving unity not by enforcing doctrinal statements like the Thirty-Nine Articles but through common worship of God's majesty. Such views helped create the idea of a "Broad" church. Coleridge also hoped that one day a "clerisy", sensitive Christian intellectuals, would form the soul and spirit of the nation. In 1840, his <u>Confessions of an Enquiring Spirit</u> were posthumously published, helping to extend Coleridge's influence even longer. Whether they agreed with Coleridge or objected to his views, early Victorian minds had to come to terms with his argument that the Christian faith and statements of Christian doctrine were very different matters.

As influential as Coleridge and the Romantic movement were, clergymen were usually concerned with more immediate issues. It was their hostile reaction to the modest Parliamentary reforms of 1833 which, combined with the Romantic climate and with the growing militancy of the High Church Anglicans, produced one of the most significant developments within Victorian religious history.

The Oxford Movement

Oxford University was Britain's center of political and religious conservatism during the early Victorian years. Many professors there were also Anglican clergymen and they were especially concerned that the law reducing the numbers of Irish bishops was creating a precedent for additional Parliamentary interference with the church. Responding to what he considered a

44

most serious situation, John Keble (1792-1866), a professor of poetry, delivered a sermon entitled "National Apostasy" at the university church of St. Mary the Virgin on July 14, 1833. He scolded Parliament for its recent actions, supporting his condemnation of the government on the grounds that the Church of England was an ancient and divinely instituted body which should not, therefore, be so lightly tampered with by Parliament.

Like Keble, most Anglican clergy were sympathetic to the Tory party and could not abide a Whig government meddling in their affairs. This particular sermon contained little that was new, but it did prove to be the beginning of a campaign. Led by a small group of high church clergymen at the University, the Oxford Movement sought to reassert the spiritual and historical authority of the Anglican Church. They exalted Christian tradition, liturgical formality, and they preached an apostolic dedication to God. Where the Evangelicals stressed the relationship of the individual fallen sinner to a saving Christ, these Oxford partisans emphasized the mission of the entire body of Christ, the Church.

The Oxford Movement was conservative because it paid so much attention to the past. In another sense, the Oxford disciples were stubborn revolutionaries, offering a serious challenge to the view that the Church (the "visible" church in theological terms) was of any secondary importance in the process of salvation.

Edward Pusey (1800-1882) was the second of the three figures who best represents the high Anglican tradition at Oxford. A professor of Hebrew, Pusey was a shy and withdrawn individual, in no way qualified to lead. He had a great love for the ceremonial and he preached a life of Christian devotion and obedience to the Church. These views gained such popularity that, by 1840, "Puseyism" had come to designate what was going on at Oxford.

When requested to define his values specifically, Pusey spoke first of his love for the mystery of the Sacraments. He believed the episcopal system was God's holy ordinance and he assigned a high status to the visible acts of devotion. In short, Pusey was a Christian mystic. His emphasis on episcopal authority in the Church and the value of elaborate liturgical rites smacked strongly of Roman Catholicism, but many an Oxford student and young clergyman gave Pusey's views positive and responsive consideration.

The central figure of the Oxford Movement was a man who far outstripped both Pusey and Keble in leadership and literary

45

ability. John Henry Newman (1801-1890) was one of the most fascinating figures of the Victorian age. Born and raised in the
Evangelical tradition, Newman entered Oxford in 1817. He was
ordained an Anglican priest in 1825 and soon became a fellow of
Oriel College, Oxford.

Shortly following Keble's sermon, Newman joined with other
Oxford scholars in publishing a series of tracts (The term
"Tractarian" is also used to refer to the Oxford Movement) aimed
especially at clergymen, calling upon them to recognize their
high offices and to see themselves as direct descendents of the
early apostles. "I fear", wrote Newman in the first of the tracts,
"that we have neglected the real ground on which our authority is
built--our APOSTOLIC DESCENT". If there was one word which Newman
had already come to reject it was "Protestant". There was but
one, true and universal Church, Newman believed, from which no
true Christian could be separated. It was in this Church, not
just in faith or in the conscience, that true security of salvation could be found.

It is hardly possible to exaggerate Newman's role as the real
leader of the Oxford Movement. Although many scholars at the
University were alarmed at his statements and condemned him for
leaning toward Roman Catholicism, Newman was not discouraged. He
challenged the criticism. Students became enthralled by him.
They flocked to hear his sermons, imitated his speech, walked and
knelt, mimicking Newman's own characteristics. The Church of
England might frown on him but it could not deny Newman his
popularity.

Suspicions of Newman's leanings toward Roman Catholicism
were confirmed in 1841 with the publication of the last of the
tracts, famous Tract Ninety. In it Newman demonstrated that the
doctrinal positions of the Church of England, as summarized in
the Thirty-Nine Articles, were not necessarily incompatible with
Catholicism. This publication brought down the official wrath of
Oxford and, in 1843, Newman left the university for the quiet of
a rural home at Littlemore, a short distance away. There he lived
an almost monastic life, devoting himself to his disciples and to
writing his Essay on the Development of Christian Doctrine (1845).

When one of his proteges, W.G. Ward (1812-1882) was deprived
of his Oxford degree for expressing adherence to Catholic beliefs,
Newman made the announcement which many had been waiting to hear.
He had become a convert to Roman Catholicism. In 1847 he went to

JOHN NEWMAN

Rome and was ordained a Catholic priest. Newman then returned to England to work and to write; in 1879 he was made a Cardinal by Pope Leo XIII. Newman not only distinguished himself by his religious odessey. He was also one of the leading scholars and thinkers of the Victorian age. His Idea of a University (1852) was a landmark in thought about liberal education and his Apologia pro vita sua, written in 1864, is one of the most important auto-biographical works of all time.

Few Anglicans had the courage to follow Newman into the fold of Catholicism. His departure deprived the Oxford Movement of its greatest leader; as an organized effort, the Movement was finished. But the Oxford Movement did have an immediate impact upon the form of Anglican worship. For example, the Sacrament of Communion became frequently rather than occasionally celebrated. Clergymen generally took their callings more seriously; they preached better sermons and exhorted their parishoners to rededicate themselves to Christian service.

Evangelicalism had given the Victorian age a new sense of personal salvation and an obligation to serve one's fellowmen. By emphasizing the corporate nature of Christianity, the Oxford Movement contributed to the slow reorienting of the Church as a whole to its role in society. Because it was concerned chiefly with intellectual and liturgical matters, the Oxford Movement was of little immediate significance to the Victorian working classes. However, direct questions about Christianity's social mission were becoming asked more and more frequently at mid-century, serious queries which could not be brushed aside any longer.

The Churches and the Victorian Poor

The figures contained in the Religious Census of 1851 were not the only bits of information relative to the state of Christianity among the Victorian poor. In 1851, Henry Mayhew (1812-1887) pre-sented his London Labour and the London Poor, a vivid sociological survey of life in London slums. Mayhew and his assistants asked people questions which delved into every aspect of their lives. In addition to all the other information obtained about the mid-Victorian poor, they discovered that the poor had precious little religious knowledge and almost no contact with church or chapel.

48

One man was asked if he knew anything of St. Paul's Cathedral.[4] "A Church sir, so I've heard. I never was in a church." It was an honest and typical response, verifying the observation that the lowest economic classes had little or no Christian awareness.

Like all other Victorian social institutions, the churches were placed under severe strains by the demographic consequences of the Industrial Revolution. No longer were a reasonable number of parishoners served by a clergyman. While some parishes were nearly deserted as people moved away, others were swollen with humanity.

Because of the nature of its decision-making structure, methods of finance, and its general attachment to conservative social attitudes, the Church of England had more than its share of difficulty in adjusting to such a different social situation. There were too few churches and seldom did clergymen forsake the relative comforts of a middle class or rural parish for the cities.

Most Dissenting congregations were no more able than the Anglicans to cope with urbanization. Congregationalists, Unitarians and Baptists drew their numbers from the respectable middle classes. Because Dissenters depended solely on income from voluntary contributions and recent endowments it was extremely difficult to survive in urban areas. As their members fled the crowded cities for suburban areas, their churches followed. Before 1850 the most active body in Victorian slums were the Roman Catholics, ministering to the masses of Irish immigrants.

The impact of urbanization on Christian institutions was most gruesomely illustrated by the failure of the Church of England to fulfill one of its exclusive responsibilities: the burial of the dead. Cemeteries became so overcrowded that graves were sometimes disturbed to make room for new corpses. Skeletons were seen to be scattered about by grave-diggers. When the cholera or other epidemic visited London, people had to stand in line waiting to bury

---

[4] In Victorian times, St. Paul's still was the largest Protestant church in the world. Its massive dome dominated the London skyline. Built after the London fire of 1666, it was the architectural masterpiece of Sir Christopher Wren.

their dead. In the interests of sanitation, the government closed down many church plots and in 1853 opened new public cemeteries, much to the discouragement of some clergymen who found themselves deprived of burial fees.

As early as 1818, Parliament had recognized that new churches needed to be built and appropriated a million pounds for construction. It became difficult, in the face of the political power of Dissent after the Reform Act, for Parliament to show this sort of favoritism. Private contributions did account for some new church construction but it was very difficult to find those willing to contribute to the cost of maintaining and staffing a new church. Moreover, even new pews remained empty. Although estimates vary, probably no more than one person in ten who lived in a poor city neighborhood attended any church or chapel.

This was a fact of utmost concern to Victorian Christians. Admittedly, it was not the obligation to save souls which prompted such worry. They troubled themselves over the uncertain morality of the laboring classes. The poor were clearly not receiving proper ethical instruction; they were not being made aware of the need to obey civil authority. Were the poor not becoming ignorant of the frightful, eternal consequences awaiting the sinner? The middle and upper sectors of British society had been certain for a long time that the poor might possibly constitute a threat to the established structure of society and the lack of church-going habits among the Victorian laboring classes only served to reinforce the "respectable" in their opinion.

Various reasons were given for the failure of the poor to attend church. A costermonger interviewed by Henry Mayhew explained why his friends stayed away from churches.

They see people come out of church and chapel, and as
they're mostly well dressed, and there's very few of
their own sort among the church goers, the costers
somehow mix up being religious with being respectable,
and so they have a queer sort of feeling about it.

Many of the poor had no shoes, they dressed in little more than rags and naturally hesitated to embarrass themselves. It would be a mistake, however, to assume that the poor were driven out of the churches by middle class snobbery. There is a good deal of truth to the observation made by one clergyman near the end of the nineteenth century when he said that the Church did not lose the great towns; it never had them in the first place.[5]

Like most generalizations this one too had its exceptions. In some regions, the Methodists retained a traditional link with the poor. Despite Methodism's growing respectability and the conservatism of the Methodist leadership, their chapels continued to draw laboring folk in areas like Cornwall and Wales. During the heyday of Chartism, the Methodists found the Chartists less opposed to them than to other denominations.[6] The Methodists, however, were not strong in London, Manchester or Birmingham.

Some Victorians suspected that a major cause of working class irreligion was the anti-Christian propaganda spread by Owenite Socialists and Secularists. The pugnacious Bishop of Exeter, Henry Phillpotts (1778-1869) had done his best as early as 1837 to have Socialists prosecuted for distributing literature about their new moral world. Although there were a number of very outspoken, itinerant "atheists", few among the laboring poor paid much attention. Nevertheless the term Socialism was associated with atheism and was considered to be a dangerous threat.

In limited ways, some representatives of the Church of England had become involved in working for better employment and living conditions for the poor. In the large cities, charity and educational societies were founded. The best representative of this kind of work was Lord Shaftsbury (1801-1885), a Tory Evangelical. Motivated by charitable impulses, Shaftsbury campaigned vigorously for limitations on hours of labor and he worked especially hard to alleviate the plight of working women and children. He and people like him were well-meaning and they did indeed accomplish considerable good. However they made no secret of their paternalism, believing that the poor man needed to be ruled by those who were his social betters. Such attitudes were anathema to Chartists, Socialists and to those self-educated workingmen who had gained a measure of independence and self-respect.

---

[5] K.S. Inglis, Churches and the Working Classes in Victorian England (Toronto, 1963), p. 3.

[6] Some Chartists founded their own churches, believing as one leader, William Lovett (1800-1877) had said, that few Christian churches actually practiced true Christianity.

In 1848, many Victorians were especially alarmed by the revolutionary situation which they believed was rapidly developing. On the continent--in France, Prussia, Austria and Italy--revolutions were, in Lord Shaftsbury's words, going off like pop-guns. Unlike the revolutionaries of 1789 and 1830, the 1848 participants demanded more than civil liberties such as freedom of the press. They also sought to achieve a measure of social equality and economic security for workingmen. After a few limited objectives were gained, the forces of reaction overcame the workers, students, and their supporters. The June Days in Paris, 1848, were as bloody as any ever seen in that turbulent city.

Economic conditions for workers in Britain were as bad as they were anywhere. Friedrich Engels has so vividly described them in his <u>Conditions of the Working Class in England in 1844</u>. All that was needed was some spark to set in motion a proletarian revolution Karl Marx (1818-1883), living in London in 1848, believed that the revolution which he had recently announced in the <u>Communist Manifesto</u> had already begun in Europe. Because of its well-developed proletariat, he was sure that similar upheavals would soon be underway in Britain. Few British Socialists in 1848 had heard of Marx. Moreover the Owenite Socialist community had collapsed in 1845 and they were now a scattered and dispirited few. They could cause no trouble but their ideas were still remembered. On the other hand, the Chartists, led by Feargus O'Connor (1794-1855), were far from being quiet. In early 1848 they seemed to present a very real threat to public order.

Working class leaders in Britain had consistently condemned the churches for preaching blind obedience to an oppressive political and economic system. They rejected those Christian beliefs which emphasized human helplessness. Therefore it was hard to escape the conclusion that working class aspirations, as defined by Socialists and Chartists, and Christianity were incompatible. But this judgement had not come to be made by everyone. Perhaps it would not be impossible to regain the working classes for Christianity and to reduce the threat of disorder at the same time if it could be shown that the goals of Christianity and those of Socialism were identical rather than opposed to each other.

Christian Socialism

The Chartists had planned a monster demonstration in London for April 10, 1848. Their petition again bore millions of signatures. Moderates among the Chartist leaders had lost face and the

52

militant O'Connor hinted that he could not restrain his comrades should Parliament again reject the Charter. Although the demonstration did take place as planned, the Charter again was rejected by Parliament. But there was no violence; the Chartists remained entirely peaceable. However, the middle classes became more alarmed than ever. The future Prime Minister, Benjamin Disraeli, had written recently in his novel, Sybil (1846), that there were two nations in Britain which did not understand each other: the rich and the poor. Despite temporary tranquility, each was now quite certain of the other's enmity.

In the midst of the turmoil of 1848 an effort was begun to construct a bridge between the working classes and Christianity. Socialism claimed to be based on a belief in human equality, cooperation and mutual aid. Were not such convictions identical with the ethics and way of life advocated by Jesus himself in the New Testament? The experiment known as Christian (in opposition to the "atheistic" Owenites) Socialism was created by the combined action of three individuals.

First, there was Frederick Denison Maurice (1805-1872) a professor of theology in London. Influenced by Coleridge, Maurice sought to make the Church of England a "broad" church. Though his liberal theological opinions would soon get him into trouble with his Anglican colleagues, Maurice was acknowledged to be one of the outstanding preachers of the Victorian era. John Malcolm Ludlow (1821-1911), a young lawyer, was well acquainted with the main ideas of European socialism, having come recently from Paris where he had been an eyewitness to revolution. Maurice and Ludlow were joined by Charles Kingsley (1819-1875), an Anglican clergyman and novelist. Moved by Christian enthusiasm and by their fear of social conflict, the theologian, the ideologue and the propagandist joined efforts.

Within a month of the Chartist demonstration, they produced a series of tracts, Politics for the People, an attempt to stir some enthusiasm among the better educated workingmen for Christianity. Ludlow wrote very intelligently, but it was Kingsley who drew more attention with rhetorical statements like "Instead of being a book to keep the poor in order, it (referring to the Bible) is a book, from beginning to end, written to keep the rich in order." These pamphlets found few readers, however, and the little publications came to an early end. A more definite strategy was obviously required.

On April 23, 1849 a meeting was arranged between Maurice and the London working class leaders. Maurice was at his oratorical best, his intense and honest appeals for their help overcoming the scepticism of the workingmen present. At a later gathering Kingsley helped to break down class barriers by asserting that he was a Chartist as well as an Anglican vicar.

Realizing that laborers were especially interested in social reforms and economic improvement, the Christian Socialist leaders founded the Society for Promoting Working Men's Associations in June, 1850. Middle class capital was gathered and put to use setting up workshops where laborers could produce and exchange goods without being subject to capitalist profits. Altogether twelve workshops were founded in London by tailors, printers, smiths and shoemakers. Edward Vansittart Neale (1810-1892), a wealthy lawyer, put his talents in the service of Christian Socialism and also advanced between ₤40,000 and ₤60,000 of his own fortune to assit the cooperative workshops.

For a time, all seemed to be going well. In November, 1850, the Christian Socialist newspaper, edited by Ludlow, was founded. His primary war was with "godless" socialism and Secularism, but Ludlow also condemned sterile, unsocial Christianity. Over and over Ludlow asserted that true Socialism and true Christianity both rested on the facts of human kinship and equality. Kingsley's didactic social novel, Alton Locke (1850), based on the life of the tailor, Thomas Cooper, was not great literature but it sold well and drew widespread attention to the movement. However, the combination of philanthropy, Christianity and Socialism proved but temporarily successful.

Maurice, Kingsley, Ludlow and Neale were not especially compatible. Maurice was more interested in preaching to the workingmen than in their workshops. Ludlow and Neale seemed mainly concerned with economic affairs and grew cool toward religion; Kingsley was erratic and easily disillusioned. The workingmen who had joined the shops also began to lose interest due mainly to the prosperous conditions of the 1850s. They simply could do better for themselves elsewhere.

By 1855, the Christian Socialist movement had died away. One very important and immediate benefit had been the winning of the Industrial and Provident Societies Act (1852) from Parliament. Cooperative societies were now permitted to pool funds in order to

engage in wholesale selling to their members. The British Cooperative Movement which had been started by a few ex-Owenites in
Rochdale near Manchester in 1846 was growing rapidly and profited
much from this favorable law. Of much more significance is the
fact that the Christian Socialists set a precedent for the future.
The idea that the Church of England and other Christian sects had
a responsibility for social and economic welfare would bear fruit
later in the century. On the other hand the failure of Christian
Socialism also illustrated a social fact of major importance: the
lean days of the 1840s had given way to better times.

The Tranquil Years - England in the 1850s

The 1850s stand to the 1840s as day from night. They were
prosperous years as wages rose and the condition of life for the
Victorian working classes generally improved although areas of
extreme poverty would long remain. In part, the prosperity was
due to the favorable impact on the economy of the railroads. Jobs
were created and commodity prices were lowered by these wonderful
iron monsters. Lancashire textile mills gorged themselves on
American cotton and exports of all British products increased as
tariff barriers fell to the doctrines of international free trade.
No other nation could compete with British industry.

Politics reflected this prosperity. Lord Palmerston (1784-
1865), the Prime Minister from 1855 to 1858 and again from 1859 to
1865 demonstrated the nation's mood by thwarting the small minority
who still campaigned for more political reform. At the same time,
he followed an aggressive foreign policy to the delight of both
conservative and liberal elements.

Even the barriers between the middle and the working classes
appeared to be weakening. The middle classes, from shopkeepers to
bankers, and their values dominated mid-Victorian society. The
cornerstone of their value system was self-help, accompanied by the
assurance that hardworking, God-fearing people could nearly always
gain success and respectability. Although the pursuit of wealth
became the only goal for some, most members of the middle classes
retained something of a social conscience. Such values were also
quite acceptable to another very important sector of Victorian
society, the upper echelon of the working class known as the labor
aristocracy. Distinguished by their skills, good wages and regular
employment, these labor aristocrats acted as a bridge between the
middle class and other elements of the working classes. Although

they sought respectability, members of the labor aristocracy did not forget that most political and economic goals still waited to be achieved.

The 1850s was also a decade of relative calm before future tempests would threaten Victorian Christians but there were a few troublesome people about. The heirs of Benthamism, remaining convinced that Christian belief belonged to the Dark Ages, continued to find hearers among well educated Victorians. Organized Secularism, led in the 1850s by George Jacob Holyoake, also attracted considerable notoriety. Although thousands of people attended well-publicized debates on the "merits of atheism" between Holyoake and adventursome clergymen, Secularism took root only among small groups of the more educated working men. Holyoake recognized that Secularism had a very limited appeal and in the lat 1850s he redirected his efforts to politics and the cooperative movement. There was also a sensitive and troubled person here and there worried about his or her faith and about Scriptural truths. It would be incorrect, however, to conclude that Victorian Christians generally were much aware of such broodings.

If one could forget about the unchurched poor (and one could do that easily in the 1850s because they were no threat to the social equilibrium) all seemed well for the churches of England. Some people worried about the increasing number of Roman Catholic immigrants and the fact that, in 1850, Pope Pius IX had restored a Catholic hierarchy in England, appointing Cardinal Nicholas Wiseman (1802-1865) as the first Archbishop of Westminster. There was some public expression of anti-Catholicism but it was short-lived.

There were few other issues for Christians to get excited about. Dissenters had the last of their civil disabilities removed when they were finally permitted to enter and receive degrees at Oxford and Cambridge. A minor fuss was raised about the kind of public activities which should be permitted on Sundays but hardly was this a significant problem. One indicator of the state of mind during the 1850s was that the reading public was amused rather that angered over the unflattering portraits, presented by Anthony Trollope (1815-1882), of clergymen in his Barchester novels.

The middle classes set the standards of conduct for mid-Victorian society and the family was the fundamental social component of the middle class. More often stern than affectionate, the Victorian father demanded the respect of wife and children. In many middle class families, children were put under the care of a nurse until adolescence, and had only limited and formal contact with either parent. It was an austere, disciplined but secure life underpinned by the frequent injunction that the first duty of the Christian child was obedience to anyone in a position of authority. The Bible was used to ingrain codes of moral conduct and images of hell remained vivid.

During the 1840s and 1850s children were taught to adhere strictly to the Scriptures as interpreted by their elders. These children would grow to maturity in the following decades--times in which religious doubt, rather than easy assurance, would be normal. The self-help ethic of the middle classes had made education an essential element to success. As would soon become evident, education--as it is in any age--is the most powerful threat to any form of intellectual rigidity.

CHAPTER IV. SCIENCE AND SOCIETY

The Challenge of Ideas

It is indisputable that the characteristics of urban life were principally responsible for separating the Victorian working classes from the simple Christian affiliations of their rural ancestors. Around 1860 another observation, based on rather more impressionistic but yet convincing evidence, could be made. Middle and upper-class Victorians--the best educated members of their society--were frequently being tormented by religious doubt. The Christian creeds were repeated Sunday after Sunday and still, for the majority of worshippers, summarized basic Christian convictions. For a growing number of people, however, the very foundations of Christianity were being called into question.

Only a few Victorians--freethinkers and rationalists--openly proclaimed their unbelief. It was more common to confide one's spiritual agonies to the privacy of a diary or in a letter to a trusted friend. The reason for such doubts is clear enough. No longer could Victorians easily reconcile the Christian teachings, which had assumed such an important place in their entire lives since childhood, with modern ideas.

Victorians had always known criticism of their Christianity for it was a product of an intellectual tradition extending back to the seventeenth century. In fact the leading authority on so many public and philosophical questions of the Victorian age was John Stuart Mill (1806-1873) and he was no Christian. Mill and other rationalists demanded that truth be derived by a rigorous logical process. Even if God did exist, they argued, He was beyond the human senses and reason; therefore, nothing could be known about God in the strict sense of the word. Because "atheist" was such a derogatory term, "agnostic" was coined and claimed by those who, with Mill, insisted that knowledge of God was really impossible.[1] Victorian Christians were not generally bothered by

---

[1] Mill's Essays on Theism, published shortly after his death, were a surprise to his own disciples. They hinted that Mill had doubts about the agnostic position and even carried expressions of Mill's hope that there might be existence after death.

59

rationalism. Confined to an elite few the agnostic position had actually done little to discredit Christianity. During the middle and later Victorian years, a variety of new developments came to generate religious doubt.

The mental picture of God which so many Victorians carried into their adult years was that of a supremely intelligent power, controlling the universe of His creation. He mercifully forgave those who had repented of their sins, believed in Christ's atonement on the cross, and who then strove with all their effort to live rightly. Unrepentent sinners, including those millions of "heathen" beyond the fringes of the Christian nations, were damned to everlasting hell. It was believed that these absolute and undeniable truths had been revealed, once and for all, nineteen hundred years before. From Genesis to Revelations, the Bible was accepted by Anglicans, high and low, by most Dissenters and by Catholics, as true in every word.

Daily and disciplined study of Scripture insured that the Victorians became the most Biblically literate people of all time. Their speeches, novels and poetry, newspapers and letters reflected both content and style of the King James version of the Bible. But knowledge had never been enough; a true Christian should be charitable in every way. Jesus was infinitely kind and it behooved his Victorian disciples to emulate his virtues. It was exactly on the question of God's justice and His mercy that the Bible-reading Victorians began to have anxiety for the image of God which they often encountered on the pages of the Old Testament became more difficult to comprehend.

Although it was clear that the New Testament displayed a God of love, the Old Testament appeared to present a God frequently bent on vengeance and given to capricious wrath. Speaking through the judges and prophets, Jehovah not only approved of crime on any number of occasions but He even ordered the most barbaric atrocities to be committed by the Hebrews. Entire tribes--women, children and cattle included--were exterminated by Israelite warriors on God's command. If God were just and merciful how could He demand that Joshua destroy all Canaanites or of Saul to annihilate the entire Amalekite people?

These Biblical accounts deeply disturbed many a Victorian Christian. William Makepeace Thackeray (1811-1863), the author of Vanity Fair and Barry Lyndon, was driven to sarcasm by what he read. "Murder then Jehu. Smite, smash, run them through the body.

Kill'em old and young." In their debates with Christians, the atheist or Secularist would invariably demand that his opponent justify God's apparently blood thirsty orders. It was difficult to do.

In addition to the incredible acts of barbarism, the sexual immorality of Biblical heroes like Abraham and David was difficult to defend. Because of their hesitancy to speak openly about sex, Victorians believed that some parts of the Bible should actually be withheld from young eyes. Although these problems with Scripture did not in themselves produce doubts about its truthfulness, many Victorians were being prepared to pay regard to more serious Biblical criticism.

With the exception of the rationalists who dismissed the Bible as a most fallible human product, the early Victorians accepted it as an inspired and errorless recording of historical events. Jesus was divine, born of a virgin; he performed miracles and rose from the dead. The Old Testament accounts of creation, the flood and the many divine interventions were also regarded as genuine. Literary critics had been examining the Scriptures for centuries, but English scholars had never given the Bible the type of scientific and historical criticism being conducted in the early nineteenth century, especially in the German universities.

German theologians had been deeply influenced by the Enlightenment and by their love of historical accuracy. Much of what they read in the Bible seemed wildly inconsistent with reality as they experienced it. A method of Biblical criticism was developed which treated the Bible as a very human product, written like any other book by people who reported what they thought they had witnessed rather than what had actually happened. These scholars argued that the Bible was inspired, not directly by the divine hand of God, but by the fervent emotions of the early believers and by the general mentality of the ancient world. In short, as far as modern nineteenth-century men were concerned, the Bible was filled with error.

The most controversial of the German Biblical scholars was David Friedrich Strauss of the University of Tubingen. His book, Leben Jesu (The Life of Jesus) appeared in 1835. It portrayed Jesus as a remarkable man who happened to satisfy the messianic hopes of poor and discontented Jews. His life and deeds as recorded in the New Testament, Strauss contended, did not portray the acutal, historical Jesus but a mythical Christ whose nature and super-

61

natural powers had been invented by those who passionately desired
a Messiah. While Strauss did not actually state that the New
Testament was untrue, he did claim that it should not be read as
a factual record of events. Miracles did not happen in the nineteenth century and neither could they have taken place in the first
century.

The full impact of such thinking came very slowly into Victorian England. Marian Evans (the real name of novelist George Eliot)
completed her translation of Strauss' book into English in 1846.
Response varied. Most clergymen initially dismissed Strauss and
his ilk as being devilish and wrong. A few, following the example
of Coleridge, argued that it made little difference if the Scriptures were found to contain some unreliable information because
the foundations of the Christian faith really lay elsewhere, ie.,
the conscience.

Prior to 1860, the English clergy itself was little aware of
such theological controversy and the laity knew next to nothing.
Only very gradually did modern Biblical scholarship come to have
an impact on belief. It was not indeed the treatises of historians
and theologians which posed the most difficult problems for
Biblical authority. The quiet "testimony of the rocks" was a far
more dangerous and immediate threat.

The science of geology had matured by 1840 from amature natural philosophy into a respectable branch of academia. In 1830,
Charles Lyell (1797-1875) published the Principles of Geology which
immediately became a widely read and standard scientific work.
Previously, theologian and layman alike believed the universe to
have been created in six days and in the exact manner explained by
Genesis. A few scholars such as the Reverend William Buckland
(1784-1856), a professor of geology at Oxford, did allow that
"day" might signify a time of great length. The age of the earth,
based on calculating the geneologies given in the Old Testament,
was fixed at approximately six thousand years. Biblical accounts
of the flood and Noah's adventures were accepted as accurate and
even found useful in explaining why marine fossils were so often
discovered far above sea level.

Lyell's Principles sought to establish the fact that many
centuries, and not a few days, were required for the formation of
existing geological strata. Based on sound research as they were,
his conclusions could not be easily discredited. But neither
could they be reconciled with a strictly literal understanding
of the Old Testament. Anyone who had come to the slightest understanding of geology found it extremely difficult to believe in an

instantaneous creation, a universal flood and the age of the earth as determined from Biblical sources. Fossilized remains of ancient creatures, now extinct, raised other difficult questions about creation and the earth's history.

Scientific investigation was a highly respected endeavor in Victorian England. No longer could the central issue be avoided. If the conclusions of geology were true then the Biblical accounts could not be taken at face value. Either Genesis had to be demoted to the status of a folk tale or new methods developed of Biblical understanding and interpretation. Some scholars, like Pye Smith, a Congregationalist, began to regard the Genesis account as expressing a real but not a scientific truth. But in the mind of the Victorian public, science and Christianity stood opposed.

Whatever interpretation one cared give to Genesis it was still axiomatic that creation, however it might have taken place, and existing natural phenomena were proofs of a divine and bene-ficent intelligence. However, Victorian Christians did not have long to wait before even those assumptions were challenged. The idea that God had carefully, by his will, fashioned each and every species of life was to be soon modified by the young science of biology.

No name has been more closely associated with the conflict between science and religion in the nineteenth century than that of Charles Darwin (1809-1882). The defenders of a narrow Christian orthodoxy or fundamentalism have villified Darwin while the apologists for science have stood him along with Galileo. As a young man, Darwin attended Cambridge University where he studied medicine and, for a time, he had even considered preparing himself for the Anglican clergy. Like his grandfather, Erasmus Darwin (1731-1801), Charles was drawn to the study of nature. In 1831, the year in which he received his degree, he was invited to accompany a scientific expedition aboard the H.M.S. Beagle to South America and the Pacific islands. This voyage was the turning point in Darwin's life and also in the science of biology.

When the expedition finally returned to England in 1836, Darwin brought a wealth of data with him. In addition to being a meticulous observer and collector of animal and plant specimens, Darwin was an excellent artist, recording in detail the features of animal and plant life observed on the voyage. During the next twenty years, Darwin used his data to substantiate the rather old notion that life forms were not static or fixed but in a continual state of change.

By the middle of the century, most members of the Victorian scientific community agreed that the age of the earth was much greater than had been earlier assumed. Victorians also accepted the Malthusian notion that all creatures, including human beings, were engaged in struggle against one another for survival. Keeping these assumptions in mind, Charles Darwin now had the evidence, he believed, to demonstrate beyond a reasonable doubt that the great variety of species were the result of natural causes and were not necessarily the product of God's intention. Genetic accidents or variations allowed some creatures to become better adapted to their environment, thus improving their chances for surviving longer in the struggle for existence. Over eons of time, genetic variation and climactic changes, coupled with the survival of the fittest, produced the entire variety of organic species including homo sapiens.

Many parts of evolutionary theory were and are still open to debate, but Darwin's careful analysis had given scientific respectability to the basic idea. He knew that such notions were likely to provoke a hostile reaction among his fellow Victorians who believed that God had separately made each species and had given His special attention to humans. Darwin therefore was hesitant to publish his views. In 1859 he did so because he received word that a fellow scientist, Alfred Russell Wallace (1832-1913) had independently reached similar conclusions. When the Origin of the Species by Means of Natural Selection was published, the excitement was keen; all 1250 copies of the first edition were sold within a few hours. The predicted reaction came almost immediately.

The church attacked. Even though liberal clergymen had overcome their fear of science, the conservatives saw Darwin as a threat. The first verbal battle over evolution was indicative of the future. A public debate was held at Oxford in 1860 between Bishop Samuel Wilberforce (1805-1873) and Thomas H. Huxley (1825-1895), a disciple of Darwin.[2] Seeking to condemn the Origin of the Species by ridicule, Wilberforce asked Huxley if he had descended from an ape on his grandfather's or his grandmother's side.

---

[2] Samuel Wilberforce was the son of anti-slavery crusader, William Wilberforce. An advocate of Tractarian views, Samuel Wilberforce was one of the most prominent Anglican bishops of the Victorian age.

Hardly could such an impertinent question suit an audience gathered to hear an intelligent discussion. Huxley's famous reply provoked both laughter at Wilberforce and sympathy for evolutionists.

> If. . . the question is put to me, would I rather have a miserable ape for a grandfather or a man highly endowed by nature and possessed of great means of influence for the mere purpose of introducing ridicule into a grave discussion--I unhesitatingly affirm my preference for the ape.

Wilberforce was beaten.

Science and Biblical criticism, and even the contents of the Scriptures themselves, combined in the Victorian age to generate doubts about many beliefs which for centuries had been considered essential to Christianity. Because of the wide-spread popularization given to scientific thought, it was not only the university graduate but the ordinary literate Victorian who came to suspect that his Christian faith was founded on ideas no longer very credible. There were those, especially the conservative Dissenters and the staunch Evangelicals of the Church of England, who demanded that Christians adhere to the old, limited interpretations of Biblical truth regardless of what the modern theologian and scientist had to say. But they preached to diminishing numbers. The fact of the matter is that greater numbers of Victorians found such controversies too far removed from life's ordinary work and pleasures to spark their interest.

For the sincere Victorian Christian, whose faith had once stood so firmly established on certain knowledge, these were times of feeling undone. Some became agnostics; others lived with their doubts. There is no better example of the sensitive Christian mind wrestling with the new ideas than that of the Poet Laureate, Alfred Lord Tennyson (1809-1892). His was poetry not for the London literati but for all the people. Tennyson's glorification of the foolhardy heroes, the Light Brigade, who charged the enemy cannon during the Crimean War, was a poem to be read by the masses, and many a Victorian committed his own favorite lines of Tennyson's poetry to memory.

Tennyson's most important religious poem, praised greatly by Queen Victoria herself, was In Memoriam. Published nearly a decade before the Origin of the Species, it already revealed the troubling religious concerns felt by Tennyson. He no longer perceived the universe to be a reflection of divine love and order; his picture was now of "Nature, red in tooth and claw". "A thousand types are gone," Tennyson makes nature cry, "I care for nothing, all shall go". It is evident that the deeply sincere Tennyson could not be certain that it was God who controlled the world. His Christian faith had lost one of its stronger props, but Christian he remained as the following lines indicate:

> I falter where I firmly trod,
> And falling with my weight of cares
> Upon the world's altar-stairs
> That slopes through darkness up to God,
>
> I stretch lame hands of faith, and grope
> And gather dust and chaff, and call
> To what I feel is Lord of all
> And faintly trust the larger hope.

He could find no use in clinging stubbornly to creeds founded on discredited facts. Later in the poem Tennyson defends those who, like himself, had to live with uncertainty.

> There lives more faith in honest doubt,
> Believe me, than in half the creeds.

Response to the Challenge

The failure of Wilberforce made it clear that Christianity could not be defended by his tactics; science was serious and had to be treated with respect. Several attempts were made, chiefly by theologians of the Church of England, to demonstrate that Christianity could live with science and modern Biblical criticism. Most significant of such efforts was the publication, in 1860, of Essays and Reviews. Based on their conviction that the clergy should neither ignore nor defame modern ideas, a small number of liberal clergymen, under the leadership of Benjamin Jowett (1817-1893) and Frederick Temple (1821-1902) produced these learned essays. They asserted that no topic was unworthy of courageous investigation because all real truth was given by God. Moreover, Christianity should be tied to no particular historical timetable. It was possible, the authors of Essays and Reviews proclaimed, to be a true Christian and yet to reject parts of the historical record and the supernatural events of the Bible.

Although Essays and Reviews was addressed to the clergy rather than the public, the reaction of Anglican officials was not surprising. The bishops unanimously declared it heretical. During the next twenty years, the exponents of orthodoxy continued to rave

66

against "modernist" theologians. For all the sound and fury, the arguments advanced by both sides accomplished little to enlighten the public. Gradually, Victorians did come to believe that they could be perfectly sincere Christians without admitting that Jonah had, in fact, been swallowed by an enormous fish.

One other incident was remarkable for the uproar it caused. The Bishop of Natal (Africa), John William Colenso (1814-1883) became inspired by Essays and Reviews, by his passion for mathematics and by the simple questions of his Zulu converts. In 1862 he published The Pentateuch Critically Examined. He challenged the veracity of various numerical figures--the size of the Israelite army during the exodus from Egypt, for example--given in the first five books of the Bible. Colenso's book could not be noted for its clarity or even for the importance of its arguments. What was astounding was that it was produced by an Anglican bishop, a man sworn to uphold the "truth" of the Scripture. Colenso seemed to be in violation of that oath and accordingly he was tried by his fellow bishops in Africa and found guilty of heresy, an ecclesiastical verdict which was diplomatically retracted when Colenso threatened to take the case into the civil courts. Colenso did not have a first-rate mind and his book was clumsy but it gave the appearance that it was now almost fashionable to attack orthodox doctrines.

During the last decades of the Victorian age, the conflict between science and religion gradually lost significance for most Christians. People had other things to think about. The fact that most Christians had adjusted their way of thinking is illustrated by the reception given a collection of essays published in 1889, entitled Lux Mundi. Issued by the Anglo-Catholic heirs of the Oxford Movement and edited by Charles Gore (1853-1932), the essays asserted that the "outlying departments of theology" needed to be revised while retaining all the essential truths of Christianity. It simply was not necessary, Lux Mundi repeated again, to read the Bible like one would read a modern history book. Although it was still an affront to the fundamentalists in all denominations, Lux Mundi was only stating ideas that had become commonplace.

By about 1890, religious doubt had either been silenced or had led to outright unbelief. The gradual loss of faith and the response of the "honest doubters" provided an important chapter in the history of Victorian ideas. But many Victorians had come to have second thoughts about more than just their religion; confidence was waning in their political and economic system as well. They also learned to worry about Britain's security in a world in which the international balance of power was shifting to Germany. The theological bickering of several decades had borne little fruit for Victorian Christianity. In the increasingly secularized world of the late Victorian age, some Christians sought new ways to revitalize their religion. The real task of the church, they concluded, lay not in arguing about doctrines but in serving human needs.

CHAPTER V. THE SOCIAL CHALLENGE

The early Victorians had seen the birth pangs of modern industrial society. Their grandchildren witnessed, in the last several
decades of the nineteenth century, industrial complexes and cities
growing painfully to maturity. Technology certainly contributed
much to this process. In 1863, London built the first underground
railway; electric lighting was introduced in 1875. That boon to
cheap transportation, the bicycle, came into use during the 1870s
and several years before Victoria's death the automobile had made
its appearance. Visionary men were predicting that powered flight
was not far in the future. The last four decades of the Victorian
era generated more changes in the life styles of great and humble persons alike than any other comparable period.

Political institutions were changing too. Although no single
piece of legislation had the importance of the Reform Bill of
1832, Parliament churned out a vast number of new laws. In 1867
and again in 1884 the franchise was expanded, enabling nearly all
adult British males to vote. In 1872 a Liberal government won the
secret ballot, which reduced the dangers of voter intimidation.
The most important result of these political changes was the
creation of modern political parties. Both Liberals and Conservatives developed a machine-like apparatus to organize the elec-
torate and unveiled popular programs to attract votes for each
party's candidates.

Municipalities made good use of expanded local government
powers. Streets were paved and sanitation systems were constructed.
Dilapidated houses were demolished and replaced with new dwellings
built by town councils. The Education Act of 1870 permitted local
governments to build elementary schools where they were needed and,
by 1891, primary education had become both free and compulsory.
Public health legislation and laws to regulate the contents of
food and drugs were enacted. The Victorians still placed high
values on individualism and self-help but it was very apparent
that more and more tasks were being collectively accomplished. At
the national and local levels the institutions of government assumed
an even larger role in social and economic affairs.

Although it is legitimate to speak of a "Great Depression",
stretching from 1873 to 1896, it was a state of businessmen's minds
rather than economic reality. Living standards continued to improve for the majority of people; housing was better, schools and
medical facilities were more readily available and opportunities

69

for relaxation increased as the normal work week contained fewer hours. And yet, prosperity did not reach everyone.

A large fraction of the late Victorian population continued to live in far below average conditions. They were most often found in urban slums; they were able to obtain only casual or seasonal employment and that for low wages. The unions shunned them and the poorest remained nearly illiterate. These unpleasant facts were partially brought to light by Charles Booth (1840-1916) who produced a multi-volumed study entitled Life and Labour of the People of London.[1] General prosperity there might well be but Booth found that nearly 30% of London's population was very poor.

Poverty had long been regarded by many a well-off Victorian as the inevitable consequence of the sinful human condition. Now a new and even more invidious justification for a callous attitude toward the poor was created. The modern social Darwinists believed that the poor represented the less fit of the human species and urged the suppression of the Poor Laws because they interferred with the natural processes of society. Herbert Spencer (1820-1903), brilliant social philosopher though he was, condemned any sort of public aid because it shifted resources from the productive to the unproductive members of society.

There were others who blamed capitalism and the private ownership of the means of production for Britain's uneven distribution of wealth. The "Condition of England" question, as it became known near the end of the century, asked whether it was right for a nation of Britain's wealth to permit so many of its citizens to go on living in such dismal conditions.

The history of the British labor movement is certainly a central theme of the later Victorian era and there is no denying that significant economic gains had been made by organized labor. Composed for the most part of skilled workers, the unions were effective in preserving gains made through collective bargaining and in preventing untimely and costly strikes. But few of the very poor were served by unions. Most union members had also made an ideological compromise. They might pay lip service to a Socialist heritage, but even when they used rather militant words when

---

[1]Begun in 1886, the last of seventeen volumes did not appear until 1903.

speaking of the "bosses", the union men of the 1880s had come to accept the premises of capitalism. The task was to appropriate, for their members, as large a percentage of profits as collective bargaining would allow.

Owenite or "utopian" Socialism had died away in Britain and had not been replaced by "scientific" or Marxian Socialism. Karl Marx had lived and worked in London for many years but his ideas had never become popular in England. The first Communist International had been founded in London but it had very little British support. Victorian workingmen placed scant importance on economic theory, believing that a fatter pay envelope was preferable to the difficult economic reasoning and revolutionary expectations of the Marxists. Marx did have one disciple in Victorian England, H.M. Hyndman (1842-1921). In 1881 he had organized the Social Democratic Federation in order to lead the workers to Marxism. Hyndman and his Federation held some major demonstrations but their abstruse programs held little appeal for workingmen and the revolutionary rhetoric of the S.D.F. proved unattractive to intellectuals.

The most significant Socialist development in Britain was the formation, in 1884, of the Fabian Society. Attracting some of the best young minds of the late Victorian era, the Fabians were dedicated to gaining the public ownership of the means of production by peaceful and parliamentary means. They conceived their task as one of educating the public and for this the Fabians certainly did not lack for talent. Early members of the Society included George Bernard Shaw (1856-1950), H.G. Wells (1866-1946) the historian Sidney Webb (1859-1947) and his equally talented wife, Beatrice Webb (1858-1943). Ultimately the greatest single accomplishment of the Fabians was the impressing on the modern Labour Party of broad Socialist goals.

During these decades when real social gains were made by some and being denied to others, it was increasingly believed that answers to fundamental social and personal problems were to be found in the natural and social sciences. Even traditional humanistic disciplines like history began to assume the trappings of science.[2] Fifty or even twenty-five years earlier a person might have sought moral advice from his clergyman but men and women of the 1880s and 1890s were looking more to science and social theory.

---

[2]When J.B. Bury took the position of Regius Professor of History at Cambridge University in 1902 he called history a science, no more and no less.

71

Christianity had become a far less important component of
culture at the end of the nineteenth century than it was in the
early Victorian age. It is not true, however, that British
churches and chapels had become mere museum relics. Especially
in the cities, individuals and small groups of Christians were
working hard to define new roles for the church.

The Late Victorian Churches and the Working Classes

It is not surprising that there was an attempt made to revive
Christian Socialism. One notable effort was made by Rev. Stewart
Headlam, a former student of F.D. Maurice. Like the early Christian
Socialists, Headlam was disturbed by the Secularists. Charles
Bradlaugh (1833-1891) had succeeded Holyoake as organized Secular-
ism's leader. Holyoake had always tried to make the Secularist
cause respectable by toning down his anti-Christian speeches.
Bradlaugh was more of a fighter; "Iconoclast" was a penname he
enjoyed. In 1877, Headlam founded the Guild of St. Matthew to com-
bat Secularism.

He soon realized, however, that the more important work was
in prompting greater concern for social issues on the part of the
Church of England. Headlam was fascinated, as were the early
Fabians, by a novel scheme presented by the American, Henry George
(1839-1897), for a single tax on the "unearned increment" of land
values. It seemed to be a just and easy way to garner public
revenue and to equalize the distribution of wealth. Headlam
worked hard for Socialist goals, for a progressive income tax and
public control of land. As a result, the Guild of St. Matthew
acquired too radical a reputation and was never able to flourish;
it attracted less than four hundred members. Headlam dissolved it
in 1909. Although it can hardly be rated a success, the Guild of
St. Matthew indicated that there was at least a little room within
the Church of England for people concerned with social problems.

A more noteworthy organization was the Christian Social Union
founded at Oxford in 1889 which sought more direct and practical
gains than the Guild of St. Matthew. Begun by many of the same
Anglo-Catholics who had cooperated on Lux Mundi, the C.S.U. was
described by Charles Gore as a "tardy act of repentance" on the
part of the Church of England. The Union recruited a membership
of over four thousand and set about dealing with such collective
"sins" as abominable housing conditions and industrial exploitation. It also sponsored the construction of settlement houses in
slum districts.

72

Political conservatives among Anglicans feared that the C.S.U. was also socialistic. Although few of its members were Socialists, the C.S.U. was so steeped in the traditions of ecclesiastical and middle class charity that it gained no workingmen as members. Perhaps the most important result of the C.S.U.'s work was that younger Anglican clergymen became more aware that the Church of England had a social as well as a spiritual responsibility.

For Catholics, the late Victorian years were decades of growth as the steady influx of Irish laborers continued. On the intellectual level Catholicism was ably defended by men like Lord Acton (1834-1902), an outstanding writer and historian, but because most late Victorian Catholics were poor and were Irish, it was natural that the Catholic Church be involved with social concerns.

Not just in Britain but almost everywhere in Europe, Catholics had a better record of social work than did Protestant denominations. In 1891 Pope Leo XIII issued his important Rerum Novarum, an encyclical which condemned both capitalist exploitation and revolutionary communism. It urged Catholics everywhere to treat one another as Christians, not just as master and employee.

Victorian Catholics did not really need this papal reminder. They had already been given an example by their Archbishop, Henry Manning (1808-1892), a convert from the Church of England who had been appointed Archbishop of Westminster in 1865. Manning was ambitious, given to conservative theological views and no friend of Newman.[3] He did have a social conscience and he liked politics. Every person, claimed Manning, had a right to the necessities of life even if that meant stealing them from the rich. By no means was the Archbishop advocating crime; he was trying to demonstrate to the rich the consequences which inevitably followed a lack of true Christian charity. In 1889, the dock workers in London went on strike. Because so many of these poorly paid men were Irish Catholics, Manning became involved and served effectively as a member of a mediating committee. Largely through his efforts, bloodshed was averted and the workers won a favorable settlement.

No development comparable to the Christian Social Union or to Manning's work took place within non-conformist churches. Hugh

---

[3]In his classic Eminent Victorians (1918), Lytton Strachey presents a brilliant but unfriendly portrait of Manning.

Price Hughes (1847-1902), a Wesleyan Methodist, sought to rid Methodism of its "no politics" label. His sermons, published as Social Christianity in 1889, asserted that poverty was less the result of sin than of social conditions. Very few other Dissenters spoke of the need for social action for it was difficult to convince middleclass congregations to abandon their commitment to individualism and free enterprise. It is striking to note, however, that many labor leaders of the time--men like Keir Hardy, Tom Mann (1856-1941) and Big Ben Tillett (1860-1943) had close ties with Dissent. Political and economic questions for these men were always associated with moral issues. Their own success as politicians depended on their ability to inspire an audience and many labor politicians had acquired rhetorical skills as youthful members of Dissenting congregations.

The late Victorian churches were slow in recognizing the fact that their nation's prosperity concealed large numbers of people who continued to live in the worst conditions. Efforts of men like Steward Headlam were always suspected of leading to socialism and of emphasizing worldly concerns at the expense of the heavenly. If the established and Dissenting churches were not going to venture into the streets where the non-respectable resided, then who would?

The Salvation Army

Oxford University customarily awards honorary degrees to individuals who have distinguished themselves in scholarship, the arts, or public service. In 1907 Oxford so honored a man who had spent most of his life in Victorian slums, a man who was still considered by many people to be nothing more than a vulgar revivalist. This degree was recognition of the singular achievement of William Booth (1829-1912), General of the Salvation Army.

Booth came from Nottingham where, as a young man, he had been converted from the Church of England to Methodism. He soon became a part-time evangelist. In 1855 Booth married Catherine Mumford (1829-1890), a member of the New Connexion Methodists and together they gained recognition as revivalist preachers, she no less than he. The Methodists, however, were not especially pleased with the Booths for two reasons. First, they were street preachers and seemed to disparage those who preferred comfortable chapel services Secondly, the Booths did not direct their efforts to the "honest" poor who made up the majority of New Connexion chapels. They went down into the underworld of Victorian prostitutes, tramps and alcoholics.

In 1861 the Booths resigned from the Methodists. The London

W^m & CATHERINE BOOTH

Quakers allowed them to preach from a tent in their cemetary and from that location William and Catherine issued their message: man had fallen into sin, he was saved through the atonement of Jesus. It was a traditional call to Christian belief but their methods were certainly extraordinary. No technique was considered too flamboyant if it gathered an audience to hear the Gospel.

Within a few years, William Booth had established over a dozen preaching stations around London. He organized his congregations into the Christian Mission with himself as General Superintendent. Women had status equal to men and all of Booth's assistant preachers were required to abstain completely from drink. Booth and his street preachers were not always treated kindly. London hooligans often made them targets of mud and stones. Some gangs were organized by brewers and tavern keepers out of fear that the "tee-total" message would damage public house business. Because the preachers of the Christian Mission were thought to constitute a public nuisance, the police often failed to give them adequate protection.

In order to attract an audience for the preacher and to drown out noisy opposition, Booth adopted a novel suggestion made by one of his assistants. Uniformed and marching "Hallelujah" bands were formed and soon became the distinguishing trademark of the Mission. The military metaphor also came into common use during the 1870s. Booth, who kept a copy of British Army Regulations at his bedside, believed that few gains were achieved by democratic organizations; too much effort was wasted in discussion. In 1878 the Salvation Army name was adopted. The War Cry began to circulate in the following year and, by 1883, 350,000 copies of the Army's newspaper were being printed each week.[4] By 1886, the British Salvation Army had over one thousand corps and some two thousand officers. Emigrating citizens exported the Army to other countries as well. There was no doubt that Booth's methods worked.

Where did the Salvation Army stand in relationship to other Christian denominations? Its work of ministering to the outcast members of society was a task which no Christian could condemn and

---

[4]The church militant was a common Victorian theme. The most famous of all militant hymns, Onward Christian Soldiers, was written by an Anglican minister in 1864.

there was nothing particularly unorthodox about Booth's theology.
But the Army's tactics--the bands, parades, tambourines and uni-
forms, revivalism--were generally thought repulsive. Booth was
honored by being asked to address the Methodist Conference of 1880,
a number of Anglican bishops were openly sympathetic to his cause,
and most importantly, the Army had no trouble in getting contributions for its work. But never did the Salvation Army escape
from the smell of vulgarity. Booth did not care.

During the 1880s a remarkable change in the Army's mission
took place. Like most other Methodists, Booth had always accepted
the notion that an individual in wretched circumstances was only
living with the result of his own sins. Having seen the very poor
first hand, Booth came to the conclusion that poverty and even
vices like drunkeness and prostitution were products of bad social
conditions. In 1890 he wrote a best-seller, In Darkest England and
the Way Out. A tenth of the population--three million people--
claimed Booth, lived miserably poor and brutal lives, many of them
chronically unemployed. Booth condemned the churches for their
contribution to such a situation and he now sounded almost like a
Socialist or Secularist. "Why," Booth asked, "all this apparatus
of temples and meeting-houses to save men from perdition in a
world which is to come, while never a helping hand is stretched
out to save them from the inferno of their present life?" The
Army began to revamp its program. Less emphasis was placed on
conversion and more on providing immediate aid for the men and
women in countless Victorian skidrows. Shelters and hostels were
built which gave free food and temporary lodgings.

Booth had an even more ambitious scheme for social regener-
ation, but it came to naught. He hoped that cooperative societies, made up of the unemployed, could be created. It was an old
dream of those who wanted to see the poor help themselves. Some
contributions did come but the cooperative societies never were
formed. By 1900 the initial fervor of the Salvation Army had
begun to decline. Although the revivalist spirit had waned, the
organization continued to recruit and to carry out its unique
work.

Booth had always desired the Army to become formally allied
with a major denomination, but this was never to come to pass.
No one disapproved of the Army in 1900 as they once had done--
even Victoria gave the Army her blessing--but it was still out of
tune with Victorian sensibilities. Even with his Oxford honorary
degree Booth was yet an outsider. Nonetheless, he and Catherine

had not failed in their work. In the words of one distinguished student of the working classes and the churches, "Nobody in Victorian England did more than Booth to put unconvention methods into the service of convention Christianity."[5]

Despite the ideas of In Darkest England, Booth was basically not very interested in politics. Most late Victorian Christians had come to compartmentalize their lives. For them, religion was a Sunday matter; politics, social questions and even personal problems were for the rest of the week.

There was one Victorian who stood out from the rest of his fellowmen because he refused such artificial distinctions. His public career, stretching from the Great Reform Bill to the very end of the century, and private life were of a piece. Even his contemporaries though he was the most eminent man of their age. He was Gladstone.

The Grand Old Man

William Ewart Gladstone, the son of a Liverpool merchant, was born in 1809. When he went down to Oxford, he was undecided whether he should enter the clergy or become a public servant. That question was resolved in 1832 when the twenty-three year old Gladstone was persuaded to run for the House of Commons and was elected as a Tory member. During Peel's short ministry in 1835, Gladstone was appointed junior Lord of the Treasury. After Peel's ministry was turned out, Gladstone returned to theological studies. The Oxford Movement was at its peak and young Gladstone was much influenced. In 1838 he wrote The State in its Relations with the Church in which he suggested that a close, almost medieval, church-state relationship was the ideal, a view which did not impress many readers.

In 1841 Gladstone joined Peel's government again and gained more financial experience as a member of the Board of Trade. When the Tories split over the free trade issue, Gladstone chose to follow Peel. During the 1850s Gladstone was courted by all poli-

---

[5]K.S. Inglis, Churches and the Working Classes in Victorian England (Toronto, 1963), p. 213.

W. GLADSTONE

tical factions. As Chancellor of the Exchequer in 1853, Gladstone distinguished himself by his firm grasp of complicated fiscal matters. Only one issue hindered Gladstone's immediate political advancement, his opposition to Palmerston's popular and hard-headed foreign policy. Gladstone believed that foreign policy issues should not be decided only in terms of serving the national interest. Every political question for him was also a moral one. The statesman had a duty to his nation but more importantly he had to do what was right.

As the Liberal party was taking shape during the 1850s and early 1860s, Gladstone became its leading personality. When Palmerstone died in 1865, Lord John Russell became Prime Minister but it was Gladstone who held the reins of power in the House of Commons. He soon electrified the working classes by declaring that every honest man should be granted the right to vote. Although it was Disraeli and the Conservatives who brought about the Reform Bill of 1867, Gladstone and the Liberals harvested the gains in the election of 1868. Disraeli might have extended the franchise, but the new voters realized that Gladstone was more committed to democracy. The Liberals won a majority of over 100 seats in the House of Commons.

As Prime Minister for the next six years, Gladstone secured major pieces of domestic legislation. He also abolished the established Protestant church in Ireland. Gladstone had no love for Catholicism, but he believed it very unjust to force Catholics to support the Church of Ireland. Of course Gladstone made enemies. In the general election of 1874, despite an impressive record of legislation, the Liberal party was defeated, drowned it was said "in a torrent of gin and beer". In his efforts to reduce the problems associated with heavy drinking, Gladstone had worked for stricter licensing of public houses. Tavern keepers and brewers, fearing their trade would be harmed, roused public opinion against the Liberals. Combined with the efforts of those who did not like his church policy or his foreign policy, their propaganda was enough to tip the scales in Disraeli's favor.

Gladstone was now sixty-five years old and had been active in politics for over forty years. He did retain his seat in the Commons but resigned as leader of the Liberal Party, a retirement which was short. Disraeli had supported nationalist movements in Turkey in order to preserve a balance of power in south-eastern Europe favorable to British interests. When Turkish nationalists massacred thousands of Bulgarian Christians in 1876, Gladstone let his feelings be known in a pamphlet entitled the Bulgarian Horrors and the Question of the East. Although some might see it as a complicated foreign policy issue, Gladstone put it simply. Britain had a responsibility to protect innocent Christians and she had failed. The old crusader just could not stay out of politics.

In 1880, the Liberals were returned and Gladstone became Prime Minister for the second time. During the next five years, Ireland became an even more important matter. Because many poor tenant farmers were being evicted, Gladstone had already, in his first ministry, secured a land reform act. It did not satisfy Irish radicals and did not stop the violence in Ireland. Gladstone was more determined now than ever to "pacify" Ireland. Out of office briefly in 1885, Gladstone returned for a third time in 1886 and presented a bill for granting independence to Ireland. Like Peel had done forty years earlier, Gladstone split his party. A large faction of Liberals who wanted the union with Ireland preserved voted with Conservative M.P.s to force Gladstone from office.

Even then his public career was not finished. In 1892, at the age of eighty-three, he became Prime Minister for the fourth and last time. With the support of the Irish members, loyal Liberals in the House of Commons did pass a Home Rule Bill for Ireland only to see it decisively defeated in the House of Lords. Gladstone resigned, leaving political life by castigating the House of Lords and bearing the knowledge that he had not succeeded in working out a just settlement for Ireland.

When Gladstone died in 1898, the Victorian age lost its greatest and its most Christian statesman. He had often remarked that his little book of 1838 was a juvenile product, but his own life had been a true linkage between the secular and the sacred.

Gladstone possessed a certain rigidity of character that made it difficult for people to feel entirely comfortable with him. Yet his political decisions were never narrow minded. As Prime Minister he appointed bishops from both the Liberal and Conservative parties, always choosing men who were very dedicated whatever their political preferences. His own liberalism was generous and is best illustrated by his support for the atheist, Charles Bradlaugh. In 1880, Bradlaugh was elected to the House of Commons. He refused to take the required oath because that involved pledging honor to a God whom Bradlaugh denied. No two men could have had more diverse religious convictions. There was much hostility to Bradlaugh both within Parliament and in the country but Gladstone supported Bradlaugh's right to sit in the Commons. Finally in 1886, Bradlaugh was allowed to take his seat.

People respected Gladstone more than they loved him. Unlike Disraeli, Gladstone was not an engaging and witty person. His announced moral standards were perhaps too high and he preached at people too often. Victoria despised both him and his Liberal politics. Great as he was, Gladstone did not quite fit into the world of late Victorian politics. While other politicians could be found relaxing at their clubs, Gladstone was reading theology or engaging in his own crusade to rehabilitate prostitutes. He sought them out on London streets and then, much to their astonishment, took them home to Mrs. Gladstone for motherly counseling. Mainly it was his insistence that political issues were also moral questions which conflicted with the rise of social science and power politics in the late nineteenth century.

Gladstone never lost his Christian confidence although like Tennyson, he could not completely escape doubt. Shortly before his death, Gladstone corresponded with the old Secularist, Holyoake, who had become a staunch supporter of the Liberal party. Gladstone knew that his own life was nearly over and he freely confessed his fear of "surrendering to the cold embrace of extinction."[6]

With Gladstone's death, the Victorian age had nearly come to an end. Although the increasing population kept existing churches well filled, the last decades of the century had been difficult ones for Victorian Christianity. Religion had become a much less important component of life and culture; and this process of secularization would gain momentum as the new century opened.

During the nineteenth century many Victorians had envisioned an entire world made Christian. Technology, wealth and cultural pride had resulted in Christian men and women being sent as missionaries into the "uttermost parts of the earth". Although

---

[6] The letters are contained in the Holyoake Collection, Cooperative Union, Ltd., Manchester.

their lives extended far beyond the island shores of Britain, they and the organizations who sent them, constituted an important feature of Victorian history.

CHAPTER VI. TO THE UTTERMOST PARTS OF THE EARTH

The Imperial Idea

In 1533 the Parliament of Henry VIII passed one of England's constitutional landmarks, the Act of Appeals. Directed especially against the Roman pontiff, it declared that all future questions, political and ecclesiastic, could be decided only within the realm. This was so, the act declared, because England was an Empire. In the sense which sixteenth-century parliamentarians understood that term, "empire" signified a sovereign state. No one had higher authority on any English matter than the King in Parliament.

"Empire" had not yet come to be defined as an association of lands and peoples who acknowledged a common ruler. Henry VIII certainly thought himself a glorious monarch and, by the standards of his day, he really was quite a figure. But compared with the vast, imperial domain of Victoria at the time of her Diamond Jubilee, a celebration marking the sixtieth year of her reign in 1897, Henry's realm would have appeared quite insignificant. His rule extended, with considerable difficulty, to a few million mostly illiterate subjects. Victoria's armies, navies and battalions of civil servants administered the lives of nearly half a billion people, one-quarter of the world's population. Tudor pennants fluttered here and there in England during the 1530s but, at the beginning of the twentieth century, the Union Jack was saluted around the world. How envious Henry would have been of his aged and dowdy heir!

The British Empire, as it had come to exist at the end of Victoria's reign, had not been the result of policies carefully planned and steadily pursued. Although the establishment of rule over far-off lands and peoples had failed to acquire the pejorative connotations given to imperialism in the twentieth century, many early Victorians did believe imperialism to be very unwise. Only in the last three decades of the nineteenth century, when imperialism became part of European power politics, did the imperial idea become popular again in Parliament and among the general public. England, of course, did have a previous history of empire building.

Early in the seventeenth century, English explorers and traders had thrust their tiny ships westward across the Atlantic to North America and the West Indies. They also sailed around the vast mass of Africa to reach the Asian subcontinent, India. The establishment of British power in India was the result of purely commercial venturing. In 1600 the British East India Company was founded and given a monopoly on trading rights with India; throughout the seventeenth century it struggled to maintain its scattered "factories" or trading posts.

During the eighteenth century two major developments affected the British presence in India. The declining power of Indian rulers led to conditions of local warfare and general lawlessness in which any type of authority was welcomed. Secondly, after years of struggle, the armies raised by the British East India Company, under the command of Robert Clive (1725-1774), finally defeated French military units at Plassey in 1757. The East India Company thus became much more than a business; it assumed real political authority throughout much of India. Its centers of power were Madras in the south, Bombay in the west and at Calcutta in the east. Englishmen often went to India poor and returned home with lavish wealth. In 1773, Warren Hastings (1732-1818) was appointed governor-general of India and he succeeded both in extending England's power and in eliminating the most serious problems of corruption within the Company. Finally in 1784 the British government itself began to assert greater control over Company activities in India.[1]

North America was a very different case. Although the original purpose of the Virginia Company, founded in 1606, was much like that of the East India Company, at that point similarities ended. Almost no English or European peoples emigrated permanently to India but thousands went to America during the seventeenth century. Economic and political grievances may have precipitated the American rebellion, but perceptive men on both sides of the Atlantic had come to realize the practical impossibilities of governing these extensive territories situated such a great distance from London.

The American rebellion taught the British a valuable lesson; a colonial empire was far too costly. In the end, the upstart

---

[1]Hastings himself was subjected to a lengthy impeachment proceeding beginning in 1788. Although acquitted of the charges of corruption, he was a ruined man.

American colonies had become a heavy millstone around the neck of commerce. The British government spent enormously trying to hold the American colonies within their mercantile empire and had failed to protect their investment. Economists advised the nation to trade around the world wherever economic advantage was found but to forge no political bonds. Their counsel, coupled with political common sense, dictated that the British Empire should not be maintained. Therefore, during the first half of the nineteenth century independence was granted to large sectors of the Empire.

In 1763, the Peace of Paris which ended seven years of European and colonial fighting turned all of Canada over to Britain. The many French settlers in Quebec did have their religious liberties guaranteed by the Quebec Act of 1774 but neither British nor French Canadians were happy with their colonial status. In 1837 minor insurrections took place which led to the important investigations made by Lord Durham (1792-1840). He advised that the Canadian colonies be given freedom to legislate over their own internal affairs. Although it did so with some reluctance, Parliament granted the Canadians independence in 1848. The way was thus prepared for the creation of the modern Canadian nation in 1867. Although complete independence in foreign affairs would not take place until the twentieth century, Canada was certainly not part of any empire.[2]

A somewhat comparable course of events took place in Australia. Beginning in 1788, Australia was used as a penal colony to which lesser felons were transported. After seven years of servitude, they were permitted to settle as free people. When it was realized that Australia could provide a good livelihood, further colonization took place by free British immigrants. By 1850 all the Australian colonies with one exception had been granted a large measure of self-government. The New Zealand colonies were also given their independence in 1852.

With the great exception of India, the British imperial idea had been shattered by the American Revolution, by other settlers

---

[2]The Statute of Westminster (1931) gave legal status to the concept of the British Commonwealth. The notion that autonomous states could pledge allegiance to the Crown and be associated on a purely voluntary basis emerged from a series of imperial conferences held in the early twentieth century.

wishing to be rid of colonial governors and by the advocates of free trade. Even before the imperial idea had expired, however, other impulses were working to revive it.

No matter how much the British may have despised Napoleon, he had provided them with an example of dedication. The soldier in Napoleon's service had been instructed, figuratively of course, to deliver a copy of the Rights of Man and Citizen to each person living under the rule of despotism. No matter how crude Napoleon's personal ambition for power might have been, the extension of human freedom was a noble and appealing cause. English men and women, no less than the French, were extremely proud of their culture and their institutions. It was easy to make the task of spreading these benefits elsewhere into an almost sacred duty. Gladstone summed the feeling up well. These remarks uttered in 1853 may be assumed as typical of early Victorian attitudes:

> It is because we feel convinced that our Constitution is a blessing to us, and will be a blessing to our posterity. . . that we are desirous of extending its influence, and that it should not be confined within the borders of this little island; but that if it please Providence to create openings for us in the broad fields of distant continents, we shall avail ourselves in reason and moderation of those openings to reproduce the copy of those laws and institutions, those habits and national characteristics, which have made England so famous as she is.

It is easy to condemn such haughty and narrow views; nevertheless it is a fact that the Victorians were quite sure their presence within other cultures could bring only beneficial results.

An individual even more responsible than Napoleon for turning British eyes beyond their island's shores was John Wesley. "The world is my parish," Wesley had claimed. His spiritual heirs, the Evangelicals--devote members of all denominations who shared Wesley's zeal to spread the Christian Gospel--accepted his statement as their own commission. During the nineteenth century, thousands of Victorian missionaries, women as well as men, would carry their Bibles and the values of their own culture to nearly every inhabited part of the world. Their task, not unlike that of Napoleon's soldier, was to liberate people from oppression, from spiritual and cultural bondage. The leading Evangelical of his day, William Wilberforce, declared that the tasks were to

> raise these wretched beings out of their present miserable condition, and above all, to communicate to them those

blessed truths, which would not only improve their under-
standings and elevate their minds, but would, in ten thousand
ways, promote their temporal well-being, and point out to
them a sure path to everlasting happiness.

The Evangelical revival in Britain spawned a number of missionary societies at the end of the eighteenth century. In 1792
the English Baptists founded a society. This was followed in 1795
by the creation, on non-denominational lines, of the London Missionary Society. The Church Missionary Society was founded in
1799 by Anglicans and, in 1804, the British and Foreign Bible
Society was created to produce and deliver the Bible in foreign
translations.

The purpose of these organizations was to raise money in
order to send missionaries, like so many St. Pauls, to preach in
non-Christian regions. Other Christians might stay behind, sur-
rounded by the physical comforts of England and argue over doctrine and ecclesiastical politics, but the missionaries wanted only
to preach. Throughout the century, most British missionaries--
and they comprised four-fifths of all Protestant missionaries--
were sponsored by these societies.

Missionaries were not much interested in British foreign
affairs or in how their own actions might effect their nation's
politics. It was extremely difficult, however, to separate missionary activity from government colonial policy and foreign
relations. Missionaries were British citizens, carried British
technology and certainly could not escape their inherited values.

The Victorian missionary might be found anywhere in the world,
from among the primitive peoples of Tierra del Fuego at the tip
of South America to the Eskimo people of the Arctic. The main
areas of concentration, however, were in the large nations of India
and China and in the unknown regions of Africa.

<u>India</u>

Despite its political authority, the **East** India Company
attempted to follow a policy of non-interference with Indian culture. In fact the company had placed a prohibition on missionaries entering their regions of control for fear that such activities might prove harmful to trade. Although British chaplains
ministered to the members of the Company, the Indian Hindu and
Moslem population continued to practice their religions without

interference. At the beginning of the nineteenth century this situation began to change.

One factor in opening India to Christianity was the work of William Carey (1761-1834), often called the father of modern missions. Like many early British missionaries, Carey came from humble origins. He was a cobbler by trade and he had little formal education and no theological training. Influenced by the Evangelical revival and his Baptist background, Carey wrote An Enquiry into the Obligation of Christians to Use Means for the Conversion of the Heathen in 1792. The next year, Carey took his family to India as the first representative sent out by the Baptist Missionary Society.

Because of the restrictions placed on missionary activity by the East India Company, Carey's work made slow progress. He spent nearly all of his time working on a translation of the New Testament into Bengali. In 1799 he joined a small group of missionaries in a Danish colony near Calcutta where there was more freedom to preach. Eventually a small college for Indian students was established there.

Carey did have very definite views about missionary work. In addition to preaching, the Christian missionary should distribute the Bible, especially the New Testament, in the native language. Indigenous churches were to be established and native Christians trained as clergymen as soon as possible. Carey also encouraged British missionaries to learn the culture of those to whom they preached. When Carey died in 1834, there were no spectacular signs of his success but the basic pattern of missionary endeavor in India and elsewhere had been established. More importantly, the attitude of the British government and the public toward Indian affairs had undergone a remarkable change during Carey's lifetime.

The British who had been to India often developed a considerable regard for Indian learning and culture. They also had come to believe that India had now fallen into an age of barbarism and superstition.

Two social practices were particularly offensive to British eyes. The widespread custom of burning a widow on her dead husband's funeral pyre (suttee) was thought repulsive in the extreme, especially when the widow was still not out of her teens. Even more odious was the society of Thugs: a secret fraternity of robbers and murderers who worshipped the goddess, Kali. Thousands of Indian travelers were strangled yearly by the Thugs in their rites of ritual murder. The East India Company Army was successful in reducing thuggism but isolated instances of it continued to be reported frequently enough to remind Christians that much work needed to be done in India before the final vestiges of paganism were eliminated.

The increasing desire of British Christians and their government to revitalize Indian culture was demonstrated in several ways. The first Anglican Bishop of Calcutta was appointed in 1814, insuring the regular supervision of Christian work. Throughout the Victorian age a number of very able ecclesiastical administrators were sent to serve in India. An even more clear indication of the new attitude about India was given in the debates in Parliament over the renewal of the East India Company's charter in 1833. The civil servant and future historian, Thomas Babington Macaulay (1800-1859), believed that the English language and British institutions would have to become widely adopted in India if progress were to be made. In almost prophetic words, Macaulay appealed to the early Victorian's deeply ingrained sense of duty?

> It would be, on the most selfish view of the case, far better for us that the people of India were well governed and independent of us, than ill governed and subject to us. . . It may be that the public mind of India may expand under our system until it has outgrown that system; that having become instructed in European knowledge, they may, in some future age, demand European institutions. Whether such a day will ever come I know not. Whenever it comes, it will be the proudest day in English history. To have found a great people sunk in the lowest depths of slavery and superstition, to have so ruled them as to have made them desirous and capable of all the privileges of citizens, would indeed be a title to glory all our own.

Put simply, India was the child. Britain, as parent, had to tend to her education both practical and moral. This confident, generous but patronizing spirit of Macaulay was to be found in many a missionary soul.

After 1833, English missionaries as well as those from Europe and America, began to arrive in India in greater numbers. British institutions, especially those of education and law began to pervade more and more of India's life. Especially under Lord Dalhousie (1812-1860), Viceroy for India from 1848-1856, the British raj, or rule, increased. Clear indication that British institutions were unwelcome was the Indian Mutiny of 1857 when Indian soldiers, called sepoys, who served in British Army units rose in open revolt. Although the sepoys outnumbered the British troops, they were easily defeated.

The Indian Mutiny prepared the way for a new phase in British-Indian relations. In 1858 Parliament abolished the East India Company and began to rule its Indian territories directly through a Viceroy and a corps of well-trained British and Indian civil servants. The crowning touch was provided by Benjamin Disraeli. He purchased controlling shares in the new Suez canal in 1875, thus providing British ships with a secure and short route to India through the Mediterranean. In 1876 he added yet another to Victoria's already long list of titles, Empress of India.

Throughout the latter half of the Victorian age, the British raj encouraged missionary work simply by enforcing the principle of religious equality. Indians who became Christian were not to suffer for changing their faith. Despite the efforts of the missionaries, the work of a number of able Anglican bishops and political help, only a very tiny fraction--perhaps one million people--of the Indian population was converted to Christianity. The rest remained faithful either to their Hindu or Moslem faiths.

The announced intention of the British government was, as Macaulay had said, to prepare India to assume self-government. But increasingly British governors and administrators behaved as if they intended to remain forever in control. Although the missionaries paid lip service to Carey's advice to let Indian Christians manage their own churches, they too were reluctant to allow independence. Not surprisingly Indians came to see the missionary attitude as being identical with that of their British governors. As the century drew to its close, more and more Indians came to resent their Victorian rulers.

Two very different events took place on June 27, 1897. In pomp and ceremony Queen Victoria celebrated her Diamond Jubilee. All the pageantry possible was mustered out for this festival of self-congratulation as representatives from throughout the British empire, including India, paraded through London. Meanwhile in India, two British officials were shot that day by an Indian nationalist. The quest for Indian independence in the twentieth century would be marked by the peaceful protest of Gandhi rather than violence; nevertheless, the dawn had broken for the Indian nationalist movement which would culminate finally in 1947.

The Evangelical spirit had helped create the British desire
to enter into Indian affairs. Although the Victorian missionary
had done little to wean Indians from their Moslem or Hindu faith,
the hundreds of Christian schools, colleges and hospitals, sponsored and staffed by missionaries, did become a part of modern
India's heritage just as did the British educational and legal
systems of which Macaulay was so enamoured.

China

At the beginning of the Victorian age, China remained as she
had for centuries--closed and isolated from foreign influence. At
least one figurative crack had been made, however, in China's wall.
In 1684, the East India Company had been given permission to set up
a depot at Canton. As population increased in Britain during the
eighteenth century, the demand increased for Chinese products,
especially tea. With the abolition in 1813 of the East India
Company's trading monopoly in China, other merchants soon began to
crowd into Canton demanding trading privileges.

The British government had tried several times to establish
diplomatic relations with the Chinese government but had met with
no success. Although Britain made no attempt to make a colony of
China, the Victorians did become very interested and deeply involved in Chinese affairs. During the nineteenth century, the
once-powerful Manchu dynasty was crumbling, bringing chaos and
a political vacuum. Local war lords, often little more than
greedy bandits, held sway in many parts of China. In economic
terms, China was considered valuable both for its products and its
potential consumers.

Like India, China had a highly developed civilization, its
philosophic and literary traditions were in many respects superior
to the European. China also represented to Christians the prospect
of millions of souls needing salvation. Unlike India, some elements within Chinese society appeared to become more open to
Western ideas as the nineteenth century wore on.

The entrance of Christian missionaries into China was brought
about by the most deplorable of enterprises. To balance the trade
in tea taken from the Chinese, British merchants began to carry
opium from India to China. The Chinese government did its best to
prevent the traffic in drugs, but the British opium dealers were
able to enlist the aid of corrupt local officials. Together they
succeeded in creating a considerable market for the drug.

A desperate attempt was made by the Chinese government in 1839 to reestablish its authority and to put an end to opium smuggling. The opium of the British merchants was confiscated; British citizens were threatened with death and Chinese ships attacked British vessels. In order to protect British citizens and their property, Her Majesty's government was forced into the unenviable position of making war on China in defense of the opium trade.

Many protests were made in Parliament and in the press against such action, all on the grounds that opium dealing was an indefensible business. The war went on, however, and the Chinese were quickly defeated. Lord Shaftsbury spoke for many in his condemnation of Britain's behavior. "Christians have shed more heathen blood in two years," said Shaftsbury, "than heathen have shed Christian blood in two centuries." In 1842, the Treaty of Nanking brought peace; it also opened Hong Kong, Shanghai and other major Chinese ports to the British.

Immediately following the treaty, the London Missionary Society and the Church Missionary Society began to send missionaries into China. These Christians were still confined to small enclaves within the opened ports and, having little to do, much of their time was spent in quarreling with one another, a common failing of missionaries everywhere. Gradually it became evident that Christianity and Western ideas were finding their way into Chinese society.

In 1851 the Taiping (Great Peace) Rebellion began, led by Hung Hsiu-Ch'uan who believed himself to be the younger brother of Jesus. The important city of Nanking fell to the Taipings in 1853. By proclaiming the end of idolatry and claiming to adhere to the Ten Commandments, the Taipings exhibited something of a Christian influence. Most missionaries realized that the Christianity of the Taipings was shallow but they hoped that the rebellion might prepare the way for the futher penetration of Christianity. As one member of the London Missionary Society, John Griffiths, wrote, "I believe that God is uprooting idolatry in this land through the insurgents, and that He will by means of them, in connexion with the foreign missionary, plant Christianity in its stead."

In reality the Taiping rebellion was an attempt to seize power from the Manchu dynasty. Over a million Chinese joined the rebels but the movement was crushed finally in 1864 by the Chinese

army led by a British captain, Charles George "Chinese" Gordon.[3]
Hung committed suicide.

Before the 1860s Victorian missionary efforts in China were
relatively modest. In 1856 the Treaty of Tientsin allowed them
complete freedom of movement. Meanwhile in Britain, missionary
enthusiasm was heightened by a religious revival directed by the
American evangelist Dwight Moody (1837-1899) who brought his
crusade to the British Isles in 1859. The "Evangelization of
the World in our generation," was the message which Moody proclaimed to his mass audiences. A young Yorkshire Methodist, James
Hudson Taylor (1832-1905) had just such a hope for China. Taylor
had already spent seven frustrating years in China and had come
away convinced that the greatest barrier to mission success was
the failure of Victorians to become assimilated to Chinese culture.
A missionary simply could not continue to live abroad like an
Englishman.

In 1865, Taylor and his wife returned to China and established
the China Inland Mission. It was a non-denominational body and all
authority lay with Taylor in China, not in the directors of a
society quartered far away in London. Taylor issued a call for
missionaries to join him and got a surprisingly good response.
Many Victorian missionaries, after the middle of the nineteenth
century, came from the middle classes and had received substantial
theological instruction. Most of the young men who joined Taylor
enjoyed no such advantages, but they did adopt the dress and, as
far as they could, the life style of those whom they hoped to
convert. Taylor and his methods have been appropriately compared
to William Booth and the Salvation Army.

Recruits to the China Inland Mission came from all over the
world. In 1884, seven Cambridge University graduates went to
join the Mission and lent it a more scholarly tone. By 1900,
China was being served by approximately fifteen hundred missionaries,
nearly half of them associated with Taylor. As they had in India,
these missionaries fell far short of reaching their expectations
for converting the Chinese to Christianity. Only a tiny fraction
of a percent of China's population became Christian and they were
despised by those patriots who wanted to restore the national dig-
nity and traditional isolation of China.

---

[3]Gordon led an astonishing career; he died defending Khartoum
in 1885.

The Boxer Rebellion of 1900 was committed to the expulsion of all "foreign devils". Many Chinese Christians were murdered and nearly two hundred members of missionary families lost their lives. After withstanding a seige of fifty-five days, the city of Peking was finally relieved by a joint military effort of Western powers. Actually, the Boxer Rebellion led to a more positive attitude among the younger Chinese to Christianity and Western culture because once again the weakness of Chinese institutions was underscored. During the first several decades of the twentieth century, Christian missionaries found themselves much more welcome. Their numbers increased rapidly as thousands of younger Chinese searched for any means to restore their nation's honor.

Such a person was Sun Yat-Sen (1866-1925) who, in 1911, became the first President of the new Chinese Republic. As a youth he came into contact with Anglican missionaries and was eventually baptized. For a time he studied medicine in Hong Kong at a hospital associated with the London Missionary Society. He did not, however, practice medicine long but turned his attention to efforts which might help create a new China. Although it is impossible to give complete credit to Victorian missionary work for instilling new political ideas in Sun Yat-Sen and other Chinese leaders, it would be equally wrong to claim that the missionaries played no part in that process.

Africa

No area of the world excited the Victorians, especially the Evangelically-minded, as much as Africa. So different was Africa from the cultures found in India and China that it acquired a special mystique among Victorians. North Africa and the coastal regions had been known for centuries but the African interior remained an unexplored, "dark" continent. Victorians viewed the interior as a vast, uncharted land, quite possibly concealing great wealth. They also assumed that Africa, south of the Sahara, was occupied by strange, uncivilized but child-like, people awaiting the liberating message of the Christian Gospels.

Liberation of Africans signified more than delivering to them the spiritual freedom brought by Christian faith. In Africa the hated trade in slaves was continuing unabated. It was largely through the efforts of Evangelicals that slave trading had been abolished in the British Empire in 1806. British ships of war now prowled the western coast of Africa seizing slave ships and setting their human cargoes free. As early as 1787, the Evangelicals had been instrumental in the creation of Sierra Leone, a colony for liberated slaves on the western shore of Africa.

Yet the slave trade continued along routes which were centuries old. Few slaves were taken west to the Americas anymore but Arab slave traders took tens of thousands of Africans each year to the east coast and hence to the Middle Eastern slave markets. Africa was not only the land of opportunity for preaching but also for liberating Africans from the vilest of human degradations.

The first British missionary efforts in Africa met with near disaster. Death took a high toll. By 1826, of the seventy-nine missionaries who had been sent to western Africa--to Sierra Leone and Nigeria--only fourteen remained alive. The rest had perished from fever and the debilitating effects of the strange and humid climate. Rather than acting as a deterrent, such adversities seemed to promote greater interest.

Political events also encouraged missionaries. As a result of the Napoleonic Wars, Britain acquired the Cape of Good Hope in South Africa. Not only was the Cape a strategic point on the route to India but the temperate climate of South Africa had long proven conducive to colonization. Dutch settlers, known as Boers, had been there for nearly two centuries. Resenting British encroachment and desiring to keep their black slaves after 1834, the Boer farmers moved north and east in the Great Trek of 1837-1844 to establish the Transvaal Republic and the Orange Free State. The Boers and British in South Africa were never friendly and eventually engaged in the Boer War, 1899-1902. Nevertheless the possession of South Africa opened a new avenue to the African interior for Victorian missionaries and also brought the issue of slavery into greater prominence.

A new chapter for Victorian missionary history was begun on June 1, 1840 in London when a great public meeting was sponsored by the Society for the Extinction of the Slave Trade and for the Civilization of Africa. The thousands who attended demonstrated how well patriotism combined with missionary and humanitarian zeal. Young Prince Albert was present as well as Peel and Gladstone. Aside from important political and church dignitaries, David Livingstone (1813-1873) was in the crowd. Unknown at this time, he was destined to become the most renowned missionary and explorer of the Victorian age.

Livingstone was just completing medical training and preparing to go to China as a medical missionary. He was an entirely self-made man. Born in Scotland of the Industrial Revolution, Livingstone and his whole family lived in a single small room. At the age of ten, David went twelve hours a day to the cotton mills. Somehow he managed to find the time and energy to learn Latin. When he was twenty, Livingstone resolved to become a missionary and began, therefore, to attend lectures on both theology and medicine at a small Glasgow college. In 1837 he applied to the London Missionary Society for assignment.

Prevented by the Opium War from getting to China, Livingstone set sail for South Africa in 1841. While aboard ship he received instruction in navigation acquiring a skill which soon would prove to be of considerable value. Upon his arrival in South Africa, Livingstone was sent north seven hundred miles to the mission site established by Robert Moffat (1795-1883) at Kuruman. For twenty-five years Moffat had worked among the Bechuana and was already well known in England for his translation of the Scripture into their language. Livingstone was not content to stay with Moffat or even in South Africa which had an ample supply of British missionaries. His ambition was to preach in areas where no other Christian had ever set foot.

Livingstone immediately began his travels--preaching, healing, making charts of the regions through which he passed and becoming acquainted with tribesmen. Although Livingstone was a gentle man, he demonstrated a physical nature tough enough to withstand his new environment. On this early venture he was even badly mauled by a lion. In January 1845, he returned to Moffat's settlement at Kuruman where he took Moffat's daughter, Mary, for his wife. It proved to be a difficult union for Mary because Livingstone, kind though he was, could hardly be called a model husband or father. His desire to explore and to preach put all other considerations far behind.

In 1852 Livingstone packed his family off to London and began a journey which would last nearly four years. He traveled north, on his ox Sinbad, until he reached the Zambesi river. Struggling westward he finally reached the African west coast in Angola. Many times he was stricken with fever and malaria but Livingstone never failed to make the most careful notes and record his observations. As often as he could he sent these reports back to the London Missionary Society. He had little idea how interested his fellow Victorians had become in his fascinating accounts of

DAVID LIVINGSTONE

African people and geography. Livingstone also encountered the
Arab and Portuguese slave traders whom he despised. Ironically
they befriended Livingstone and nursed him back to health on
several occasions when he was near death and without hope of
survival.

In the autumn of 1854, Livingstone began his return eastward
through central Africa. He found the great falls on the Zambesi
river and named them for his Queen. The journey was unbelievably
difficult but, despite illness and mental depression, Livingstone
marched on. Finally he arrived at Africa's east coast in May,
1856 where he soon boarded a vessel of the Royal Navy and set off
for England.

Livingstone was given a reception fitting for visiting
royalty. He was awarded a medal from the Royal Geographic Society,
the freedom of the City of London and a fellowship in the Royal
Society. When he finished his book in 1857, <u>Missionary Researches
and Travels in South Africa,</u> it sold thirteen thousand copies in
advance.

Livingstone had become <u>the</u> hero of Victorian England, com-
bining the qualities of saint, scientist and adventurer. People
found his forceful personality irresistable. On December 4, 1857
Livingstone delivered a stirring sermon in Cambridge which provided
a fitting climax to his stay in England. It was especially the
slave trade that concerned and angered him.

> I beg to direct your attention to Africa. I know that
> in a few years I shall be cut off in that country which
> is now open. Do not let it be shut again. I go back to
> Africa to try to make a path for commerce and Christianity.
> Do you carry on the work which I have begun. I leave it
> with you.

Livingstone's connection between commerce and Christianity has
been held against him by those who see conspiratorial ties between imperialist exploitation and the missionary. He honestly
believed, as did his contemporaries, that free trade would put
an end to war and to the slave trade as well by making the traffic
in slaves no longer profitable.

The Cambridge audience was electrified by the speech. From
that time on, the Victorians poured increasing numbers of men and
women and money into African missions. Many thousands of people
throughout Britain in fine country homes and in stifling city

hovels, each week contributed sums, large and small, to support
the work.

Two months later, Livingstone was back in Africa beginning
another missionary venture. Mary went along and died there in
1862. Again and again Livingstone, accompanied this time by
several fellow missionaries, saw the slave trade in operation.
He returned again to England in 1864 in order to excite the public
against the Portuguese who, although officially opposed to slaving,
turned a blind eye to the trade. In Britain, Livingstone's violent denunciations of Portugal became something of an embarrass-
ment to his government. But Livingstone did not stay long. He
was no longer comfortable in civilization and besides, like other
explorers of the time--Richard Burton (1821-1890) for example--
Livingstone hoped to discover the source of the Nile.

Following his return to Africa no news was heard of Livingstone for several years. Was he alive or had he perished? These
were the most difficult of all his travels. Years of physical
hardship had weakened Livingstone but had not crippled his resolve
to always press on. He pushed until he could go no further,
stopping in 1871 at Ujiji on the eastern shore of Lake Tanganyika.
Here the stage was set for the most dramatic meeting of the
Victorian age.

On 10 November 1871, the brash, young Welsh-American news-
paperman, Henry Morton Stanley (1841-1904) strode into Ujiji and
confronted the old white man. "Dr. Livingstone, I presume."
Stanley found more than a good story for the New York Herald. He
stayed with Livingstone four months and was deeply influenced by
the dedicated old doctor. Although he was in very poor condition,
Livingstone set out again in search of the Nile. On May 1, 1873
he was found kneeling beside his bedside, dead. His heart was
buried in Africa and his embalmed body taken to London where,
nearly a year later, it was laid in Westminster Abbey. No one
had done more than David Livingstone to put Africa into the
Victorian consciousness. His own accomplishments were astounding;
his reputation, manufactured and amplified in countless sermons
and periodicals, was even more so.

At the time of Livingstone's death, European nations were on
the verge of their "scramble" for African colonies. By 1900 nearly
all African territory would be under the direct control of the
French, Germans, Belgians and English. Through treaty and conferences the great continent was carved and divided. The slave trade
was finally brought to an end but new forms of economic exploita-

tion were often introduced as gold and diamonds were discovered.
Each European nation had its chief proponent of African imperialism
but none was more determined than Britain's Cecil Rhodes (1853-
1902). He dreamed of British possessions stretching in an unbroken
line from Cairo to the Cape.

Victorian missionaries went to Africa in larger numbers during
the age of imperialism. The African mystique was mostly responsible for this upsurge of interest. Perhaps the increasing problems confronting religion in late Victorian England--science,
materialism, etc.--also led many Christians to concentrate on
foreign mission work.

Too often, however, the late Victorian missionary was infected
by the notions of Social Darwinism. The sense of cultural superiority over the African was frequently given a racist base. A few
missionaries confessed that, in their opinion, black Africans could
never be anything more than savages. Missionaries did build
schools and, to their credit, they struggled to resist the worst
forms of exploitation brought to Africa by traders and business
interests. It cannot be denied, however, that most missionaries
sought often to change radically, even to destroy, what they
falsely assumed was a primitive or debased culture.

The prevailing late Victorian attitude to the African people
was perhaps summed up best by Sir Harry Johnston (1858-1927). He
was not a missionary but a colonial administrator and author of
some forty books on Africa. Speaking to the people of Uganda in
1900 through a missionary interpreter, Johnston said:

Tell them how interested the Queen is in their welfare,
how she wants them to improve themselves and their country.
We were like you long years ago, going about naked. . .with
our war-paint on, but when we learnt Christianity from the
Romans we changed to become great. We want you to learn
Christianity and follow our steps and you too will be great.

The pomposity of such attitudes is shocking, but Christian missionaries in Africa did succeed in winning a higher percentage of converts than did their counterparts in India and China. They made
their own contribution to the development of nationalist aspirations among Africans. Victorian missionaries may have been guilty
of teaching Africans to undervalue their own culture but they did
indeed bring Christianity to Africa as was their goal and they
helped to foster a desire for self-determination.

102

Regardless of how the total Victorian mission effort may be
judged, individual missionaries often did serve out of honest
concern for African people. This frequently meant the sacrifice
of their own lives. In 1958 President Nkrumah of Ghana depicted
the fate of many a Victorian missionary.[4]

You will often find as you travel along the roads, little
cemeteries lost in the bush where lie buried the brave men
and women who in bringing faith to this country gave the
last full measure of devotion. They knew that they faced the
certainty of loneliness and the imminent risk of death.
Yellow fever decimated them and their families. But still
they came.

Assessment

In 1901 Victorian missionary societies had an annual income
in excess of one and one-half million pounds which they used to
sponsor nearly 4500 missionaries around the world. During the
previous century many hundreds more had gone out from Britain to
distant places. Such an impressive record was this that church
historian Kenneth Scott Latourette devoted two immense volumes in
his History of the Expansion of Christianity to missionary work of
the nineteenth century.[5] He believed it had been "great century"
for Christianity because of its extension from Western Civilization to the rest of the world. Few scholars now would share his
views. Christianity did not become widely established in India or
China and only marginally elsewhere.

Other historians have emphasized the connection between the
cultural imperialism of missionary efforts with the economic and

---

[4] Kwame Nkrumah (1909-1972) led the struggle for Ghana's
independence, serving first as Prime Minister, then President from
1960-1966. Although he introduced a number of authoritarian measures, Nkrumah was one of Africas leading Marxists and spokesman
for Black nationalism.

[5] K.S. Latourette, History of the Expansion of Christianity,
Vols. V and VI (London, 1943).

political domination of Western nations. While the Victorian missionary kept the spiritual and the political welfare of his little flock at heart, he was often helping to prepare the way for traders, adventurers and empire builders. By exalting their own Victorian institutions, missionaries undermined those of indigenous peoples, thus rendering them more open to control by foreigners.

But the Victorian missionary must not be thought of as a cause of imperialism. Given the technological difference between Western nations and the rest of the nineteenth-century world, and the European economic and political climate of the late Victorian age, there is little question that imperialism would not have taken place. Although the missionaries contributed to colonization they also helped to protect native peoples and to implant those ideas which would later be used to throw off colonial rule.

The motives of the Victorian missionaries were mixed. Their statements that their only desire was to preach Christianity should not be taken at face value. They did feel a divine calling to be sure, but they also were drawn to Africa, to Asia and to remote island stations by a thirst for adventure and the need to give a sense of meaning to their own lives.

Missionaries were certainly prone to look at an Indian, an African or Polynesian as childlike or even as a debased individual, but never as a potential beast of burden. Livingstone himself expressed how the Evangelical spirit of duty and the sense of cultural superiority were so easily mingled. Speaking of the mission enterprise in Africa, he said

> We come among them as members of a superior race and servants of a Government that desires to elevate the more degraded portions of the human family. We are adherents of a benign holy religion and may by consistent conduct and wise, patient efforts become harbingers of peace to a hitherto distracted and trodden down race.

It is this mixture of attitudes about themselves--superior yet servants--and about their potential fellow Christians--degraded, down-trodden yet members of the human family--which annuls any final judgement on the Victorian missionary.

CONCLUDING NOTE

> God of our fathers, known of old
> Lord of our far-flung battle line,
> Beneath whose awful Hand we hold
> Dominion over palm and pine--
> Lord God of Hosts, be with us yet,
> Lest we forget--lest we forget!
>
> The tumult and the shouting dies;
> The Captains and the Kings depart:
> Still stands Thine ancient sacrifice,
> An humble and a contrite heart.
> Lord God of Hosts, be with us yet,
> Lest we forget--lest we forget!

Recessional, 1897

Rudyard Kipling

In spite of being so well known for his imperialist-flavored tales and poetry, Rudyard Kipling (1865-1936) did not possess literary talents to the degree of a number of his Victorian predecessors. He composed Recessional for the Jubilee celebrations of 1897, a verse important less for its poetic merit than for the moral lesson Kipling wanted to give his countrymen. In the manner of a Hebrew prophet, he reminds them not to forget God in their day of triumph.

It was indeed a sign of the times that Kipling believed it necessary to use his position as a pulpit. So many changes-- economic revolution, political and social upheavals--had taken place during Victoria's long reign. Of equal significance certainly was the fact that British people from all stations in society had steadily become less disposed to observe the Christian faith and duties of their ancestors. This observation bothered Kipling but, in the Victorian twilight, such worriers had themselves become fewer.

It is as meaningless to claim that the Victorian age came to an end when Victoria was laid beside her beloved prince as it is to think that the era began exactly on the day she had been proclaimed Queen. If any date can be selected as that which brought down the

QUEEN VICTORIA

curtain of the Victorian world, it is August, 1914. Then the
technology of European nations, having already forged the artil-
lery, machine guns, bombs and poison gas, became the terrible
sword on which Englishmen, the French, Germans and Russians,
impaled themselves and their institutions.

The short span of years between Victoria's death and the
beginning of the First World War--the Edwardian Era--saw the
continuation of many changes. After nearly twenty years in the
political wilderness, the Liberal party was returned to power in
1906 and proceeded to enact a sweeping legislative program of
social security, health insurance, workman's compensation and much
more. These measures laid the foundations for the modern British
welfare state but it is, of course, possible to find precedent
for the Liberal program as far back as the Factory Acts of the
1840s and the reform legislation of both Gladstone's and Disraeli's
ministries.

The Edwardian era also witnessed an increase in political
tensions. Ireland continued to seeth with sectarian hatreds and
violence; the number of strikes in Britain climbed rapidly as
union leaders became more defiant toward their employers; feminists
used disruptive tactics to demand enfranchisement for women, a
goal won finally after the war in 1918. Among the more prosperous
members of Edwardian society the good life continued, tinged, however, with a longing for meaning. Only a few people actually
knew of the complex alliance systems and the growing stockpiles
of armaments throughout Europe, but many came to anticipate an
international conflict which might break the pleasant tedium of
their lives. How blind they were to the coming holocaust of the
Great War!

The Edwardian churches, most especially the Church of England,
continued to find their popularity eroded. It even became difficult to recruit enough young men for the Anglican clergy because
careers in business, civil service and education proved increasingly attractive. While the majority of Edwardians crowded their
lives with a variety of material and practical pursuits, intellectuals and academics were no longer hesitant to announce that
Christian belief and churches belonged to a historic age which
existed no longer.

The estrangement of the late Victorian and Edwardian intellectual from Christianity had generally been prompted by the belief
that natural and social science and psychology could be relied
upon to resolve most human problems. Positivism had been intro-

duced into Britain from France during the mid-nineteenth century. Although few people were induced to join Positivist societies, the ideas of Positivism's founding figure, Auguste Comte (1789-1857) were highly regarded. He had written of the organic progress of the human race from a religious age through a philosophical period, finally reaching its apex in the Positivist age of reason and science. Blissfully unaware of the future terrors of the twentieth century, late Victorians saw here a simple and believable pattern of history. Recognizing that religion did have important social functions, Comte had substituted the worship of humanity for that of God.

The events of 1914 would point out so clearly the weaknesses of parliamentary government, capitalism and Christianity. But science and its highly prized method for discovering truth would also be victims of the Great War.

By the end of the Victorian age, Christian history had completed something of a cycle. In the middle of the Age of Reason, John Wesley had preached the possibilities of Christian faith. His spiritual descendents during the earlier years of the nineteenth century, especially the Evangelicals and the Oxford "Apostles", gave a distinctive Christian flavor to their world. But the Industrial Revolution had meanwhile unleashed such a variety of circumstances that Victorian Christians were forced to fight a series of holding actions during the last fifty years of Victoria's reign, battling to conserve their intellectual credibility and to offer their society a variety of utilitarian services.

At the end of the century, Kipling's "Captains and Kings" were preparing to depart on their missions of destruction. The ancient Christian sacrifices were still being quietly if less frequently offered; the creeds were being repeated but with generally less confidence. On the whole, the churches, like the Queen, seemed to have grown old, feeble, and in search of renewal. That quest goes on even yet.

SUGGESTIONS FOR FURTHER READING

A vast number of works exist on the Victorian age and on religion. The following list is deliberately confined to a small selection of works which are especially helpful. The reader in search of additional works is advised to consult the American Historical Association's Guide to Historical Literature (1961) and Josef Altholz's fine bibliographic guide, Victorian England 1837-1901 (1970). The latter includes the most important literature published before 1968. Many of the works listed below also contain useful bibliographies.

General Histories

Arnstein, Walter. Britain Yesterday and Today: 1830 to the Present, 1966.
Briggs, Asa. The Age of Improvement, 1783-1867, 1959.
Ensor, R.C.K. England, 1870-1914, 1936.
Kitson Clark, George. The Making of Victorian England, 1962.
Perkin, Harold. The Origin of Modern English Society, 1780-1880. 1969.
Webb, Robert K. Modern England: from the eighteenth century to the present, 1968. An excellent survey with useful appendices.
Young, George M. Victorian England: Portrait of an Age. 2nd ed., 1953. Originally published in 1936, Young's masterful analysis is of extraordinary quality.

General Works on Victorian Christianity

Altholz, Joseph. The Churches in the Nineteenth Century, 1967.
Bowen, Desmond. The Idea of the Victorian Church, 1968.
Chadwick, Owen. The Victorian Church 2 vols., 1966-1970. This is the absolutely basic work on Victorian Christianity although Chadwick unfortunately has nothing to say about the missionaries.
Davies, Horton. Worship and Theology in England Vol. III-IV. Mainly liturgical history.
Elliot-Binns, Leonard, Religion in the Victorian Era, 1936.
Kitson Clark, George. Churchmen and the Condition of England, 1832-1885, 1973.

Latourette, Kenneth Scott, A History of the Expansion of Chris-
    tianity, see especially Vols. 5 and 6, 1943-44.
Marty, Martin E. The Modern Schism, 1969. See especially
    Chapter III.
Vidler, Alec. The Church in an Age of Revolution, 1961. Volume
    V in the Pelican Series on the History of the Church.

Selected Special Studies:

Armstrong, Anthony. The Church of England, the Methodists and
    Society, 1700-1850, 1973.
Backstrom, Philip. Christian Socialism and Cooperation in
    Victorian England, 1974.
Best, G.F.A. Temporal Pillars: Queen Anne's Bounty, the
    Ecclesiastical Commission and the Church of England, 1964.
Blake, Robert, Disraeli, 1966.
Bradley, Ian. The Call to Seriousness: The Evangelical Impact
    on the Victorians, 1976.
Chadwick, Owen (ed.) The Mind of the Oxford Movement, 1960. A
    fine introduction and a good collection of original writing.
Cockshut, A.O.J., Religious Controversies of the Nineteenth
    Century, 1966.
Cockshut, A.O.J., The Unbelievers, English Agnostic Thought, 1840-
    1890. 1964.
Crowther, Margaret, Church Enbattled: Religious Controversy in
    Mid-Victorian England, 1970.
Fairweather, Eugene, The Oxford Movement, 1964.
Faber, Geoffrey, Oxford Apostles, 2nd ed. 1936.
Gillespie, Charles C. Genesis and Geology: The Impact of
    Scientific Discoveries upon Religious Belief in the Decades
    Before Darwin, 1959.
Groves, Charles P. The Planting of Christianity in Africa.
    1948-1954.
Grugel, Lee. George Jacob Holyoake, 1976.
Harrison, J.F.C., Quest for the New Moral World, 1969. A study
    of the Owenites.
Inglis, Kenneth S. Churches and the Working Classes in Victorian
    England, 1963. An excellent work.
Isichei, Elizabeth. Victorian Quakers, 1970.
Longford, Elizabeth. Queen Victoria: Born to Succeed, 1964.
Magnus, Philip. Gladstone, a Biography, 1954.
Martin, David. A Sociology of English Religion, 1967. See the
    first chapter.

Moorhouse, Geoffrey, The Missionaries, 1973.
Neill, Stephen. Colonialism and Christian Missions, 1966.
_____. A History of Christian Missions, 1964.
    Vol. VI in the Pelican Series.
Reardon, B.M.G. From Coleridge to Gore: a century of Religious
    Thought in Britain, 1971.
_____ ed. Religious Thought in the Nineteenth Cen-
    tury, 1966.
Seaver, George. David Livingstone, His Life and Letters, 1957.
Semmel, Bernard. The Methodist Revolution, 1973.
Soloway, R.A. Prelates and People, Ecclesiastical Social Thought
    in England, 1783-1852, 1969.
Symondson, Anthony (ed), The Victorian Crisis of Faith, 1970.
Thompson, Kenneth. Bureaucracy and Church Reform, 1970.
Warren, Max. The Missionary Movement from Britain in Modern
    History, 1965.

Index

Albert, Prince, 16, 97
Anglican (See Church of England)
Arnold, Matthew, 11

Baptists, 32, 89
Bentham, Jeremy, 8
Blake, William, 43
Bloomfield, C.J., 41
Booth, Catherine, 74-77
Booth, Charles, 70
Booth, William, 74-78, 95
Bradlaugh, Charles, 72, 81, 82
Bright, John, 32
Bunting, Jabez, 29

Carey, Matthew, 90
Carlile, Richard, 34
Catholic Emancipation, 8
Catholics and Catholicism, 21,
    22, 32, 42, 73
Census, Religious, 34-35
Chartism, 10, 52
Christian Social Union, 72, 73
Christian Socialism, 52, 53, 54,
    55
Church of England, 20, 21, 22
    23, 24, 26, 38, 42, 72, 73,
    89, 107
Colenso, John William, 67
Coleridge, Samuel Taylor, 42,
    43, 44
Colonies (See Imperialism)
Comte, Auguste, 108
Congregationalists, 31

Darwin, Charles, 63, 64
Disraeli, Benjamin, 12, 16, 53
    80, 107
Dissenters, 21, 22, 26, 28, 30,
    34, 65

Engels, Friedrich, 52
Essays and Reviews, 66, 67
Evangelicalism, 26, 27, 65,
    93, 96

Fabian Society, 71
Fox, George, 32

Gladstone, William, 12, 16
    78-83, 88, 97, 107
Gore, Charles, 67
Guild of St. Matthew, 72

Headlam, Stewart, 72
Henry VIII, 19, 20, 85
Holyoake, George, Jacob, 34,
    56, 72
Hughes, Hugh Price, 73, 74
Huxley, Thomas, 64
Hyndman, H.M., 71

Imperialism, 12, 13, 85-89
Industrial Revolution, 2, 3,
    4, 28
    social consequences of, 5,
    6, 7
    political consequences of,
    7, 8
Ireland, 12, 80, 81

Johnston, Harry, 102
Jowett, Benjamin, 66

Keble, John, 45
Kilham, Alexander, 29
Kingsley, Charles, 53, 54
Kipling, Rudyard, 105, 108

Livingstone, David, 97-101, 104
Ludlow, John, Malcolm, 53, 54